Doubletalking
the Homophonic Sublime

Series Editors

GEORGE QUASHA
SUSAN QUASHA
CHARLES STEIN
SAM TRUITT

In Matrices

Awareness Inside Language
George Quasha in conversation with Thomas Fink

Doubletalking the Homophonic Sublime
Comedy, Appropriation, and the Sounds of One Hand Clapping
Charles Bernstein

Everything That Seems Must Seem To Be
Initial Writings from a "Parmenides Project"
Charles Stein

Doubletalking
the Homophonic Sublime

COMEDY, APPROPRIATION, AND THE
SOUNDS OF ONE HAND CLAPPING

—m—

CHARLES BERNSTEIN

MATRICES #2

First published in *Sound/Writing: On Homophonic Translation*, ed. Vincent Broqua and Dirk Weissmann (Paris: Éditions des archives contemporaines, 2019).

MATRICES
is a series of short interim editions of poetics thinking,
published under the auspices of
Station Hill of Barrytown,
a project of the Institute for Publishing Arts, Inc.,
a not-for-profit tax-exempt corporation, 501(c)(3),
120 Station Hill Road
Barrytown, NY 12507

www.stationhill.org

Design and typesetting: Susan Quasha

ISBN: 978-1-58-177194-7

Doubletalking the Homophonic Sublime

COMEDY, APPROPRIATION, AND THE SOUNDS OF ONE HAND CLAPPING[1]

> Who am I? I am not a straight stonemason,
> Neither a shipbuilder, nor a roofer,
> I am a double-dealer, with a double soul,
> A friend of night, and a daymonger.
>
> —OSIP MANDELSTAM[2]

> He speaks in six known and six unknown languages.
>
> —DANIIL KHARMS[3]

1. Sound Writing

Never met a pun I didn't like.

I'm a veritable Will Rogers, with plenty of *roger* but without the will to say *enough's enough already*. All instinct. Like a Brooklyn Ahab stalking a whale in the back yard or a curmudgeonly Odysseus hurtling toward his sirens.

But wait a sec.

This is not the opening of a nightclub act.

Jokes are not arguments.

I am for avant-garde comedy and stand-up poetry.

That is, to my way of seeing it, there are only two kinds of writing:

---

[1] First presented on November 17, 2016 at École Normale Supérieure, Paris, as the keynote for "Sound / Writing: On Homophonic Translation," an international trilingual colloquium, organized by Vincent Broqua and Dirk Weissmann. Translated by the author from Esperanto, "Duoble-Parolas la Homofonia Sublima: Komedio, Alproprigo, kaj la Sonoj de Unu Mano Kunfrapante." An audio-visual supplement (ppt), including easy links to some of the works discussed, can be downloaded at writing.upenn.edu/ezurl/10/

[2] "The Slate Ode" (1923) translated by Ian Probstein in *The River of Time: Time-Space, History, and Language in Avant-Garde, Modernist, and Contemporary Russian and Anglo-American Poetry* (New York: Academic Studies Press, 2017), p. 108.

[3] "From the Notebooks, Mid-1930s" in *Russian Absurd: Selected Writings*, tr. Alex Cigale (Evanston, IL: Northwestern University Press, 2017), p. 104.

Sound and unsound.[4] Stand-up and stand-down. Wanted and spurned. Risible and bereft. Incomprehensible and desperate. Performed and blank.

What a glorious idea Truman Capote had for typing that wasn't writing, as he said of Jack Kerouac in 1959 on David Susskind's TV show (Capote meant it as an insult).[5]

Can there be verbal sound without meaning? Soul without soul-lessness? Body without flesh? Listening without hearing? Hope sans history?

But this is going too fast.

Let me start at the beginning.

When Vincent Broqua asked me to come to Paris for a conference on homophonic translation (not *homophobic*, don't even THINK of that here!), he proposed to call it "Sound—Translation—Writing." I suggested "sound/writing"[6]: "the sturdy resources of [the] ear," as Robert Creeley once wrote me, echoing Charles Olson's "by ear, he sd."[7]

"Homophonic translation" is a genre of "sound/writing." Sound/writing provides a broader context for the homophonic imaginary and includes modernist European sound and *zaum* poetry and within the larger context of radical translation, what Haroldo de Campos calls *transcreation*[8] and Ezra Pound calls *traduction* (in the sense of *transduction*).

---

[4] "Thelonious Monk and the Performance of Poetry," in *My Way: Speeches and Poems* (Chicago: University of Chicago Press, 1999), p. 22.

[5] The source for this quote is provided at <quoteinvestigator.com/2015/09/18/typing/>.

[6] Vincent Broqua and Bernstein, email exchange, Oct. 14, 2015.

[7] "One thing to me instantly attractive is the sturdy resource of your ear, as Williams would say … ," Creeley wrote to me on Feb. 6, 1979, responding to *Shade*. The letter is included in *Selected Letters of Robert Creeley*, ed. Rod Smith, Peter Baker, and Kaplan Harris (Berkeley: University of California Press, 2014), p. 350. But there is typographical error in the published version, close to the kind of dyslexic inversion I often make: "the sturdy resources of your era," which recalls Zukofsky's paean, at the beginning of *"A"*- 22, to the errors of the ear: "An era / any time / of year" (*"A,"* also from University of California Press, 1978; reprinted by New Directions in 2011). Olson's ear line is from "I, Maximus of Gloucester, to You" (1953); see the typescript at <charlesolson.org/Files/Max1appendices/AppendixD.html>.

[8] See K. David Jackson, "Transcriação / Transcreation: The Brazilian Concrete Poets

Pound often avoided using the verb 'to translate,' preferring a calque such as 'to bring over' that recalls the etymology of the conventional term. When his first translation of Cavalcanti's "Donna mi prega" appeared in *The Dial* in 1928, he called it a "traduction," replacing the usual word with a Latinism derived ultimately from traductio, "a leading across."[9]

—*Calque* is a loan-translation, a word-for-word carrying over from one language to another (as *vers libre* to *free verse*), from the French *calquer*, to trace.

Homophonic translation is a form of sound tracing.

(My term is echopoetics.)

The homophonic sublime is a form of *délire* in Jean-Jacques Lecercle's sense, either phony or toney, depending on how you frame it.[10] At its core, homophonic translation refuses a Cartesian split between sound and sense, seeing sense as never more than an extension of sound. At every moment it refutes the idea that meaning can be displaced from sound or that reference has an arbitrary, rather than motivated, relation to acoustic rhythm, sound patterning, and aural iconicity.

From a pragmatic point of view, any individual poem will fall short of the homophonic sublime. In that sense, homophonic translations might be heard as pushing in a direction, correcting a course, re-embodying the word. The homophonic is poetry that leads by the ear, foregrounding aurality: poetry that resists cutting the umbilical c(h)ords between translated and translation, source and target, original and copy, essence and accident, brain and mass, figure and ground, spirit and materiality, irony and sincerity, singer and song, imaginary and real, semantic and antic. The homophonic sublime is a necessary improbable of poetry, a rebuke to rationality in the name of linguistic animation.

and Translation" in *The Translator as Mediator of Cultures*, ed. Humphrey Tonkin and Maria Esposito Frank (Amsterdam: John Benjamins Publishing Company, 2010).

[9] David Anderson, "Editor's Introduction," *Pound's Cavalcanti* (Princeton: Princeton University Press, 1983), p. ix.

[10] See Lecercle's essay in *Sound / Writing: On Homophonic Translation,* ed. Vincent Broqua and Dirk Weissmann (Paris: Éditions des archives contemporaines, 2020).

In its archetypical form, homophonic translation creates a perfect mirror of the sound of the source poem into the target poem. It is mimesis by, and as, other means. While homophonic translation is related to sound poetry, the premise is that it extends an original text into a new language using real, not made-up, words of the target language. In a Borgesian pluriverse, the ideal homophonic translation would be heard by the speakers of the source language as if it were the original poem while heard by the speakers of the target language as a strange word concoction but still in their own tongue. I tried this with "Sane as Tugged Vat, Your Love," my 1993 homophonic translation of Leevi Lehto's "Sanat tulevat yöllä" ("Word Arrive by Night):[11] Finnish speakers hear it as if it is their own language, yet they cannot make out the words:

Olen sanonut tästä jo monta kertaa.
Talon jokaisessa veeseessä on valo.
Sillat virtaavat itään.
Sanat tulevat yöllä koputtamatta.

O when sanity tasted of muffled curtsy.
Talon — Jokasta's vivisected valor.
Silly virtual item.
Sane as tugged vat, your love, kaput.

I've said about this many times before.
In every toilet of the house there is a light on.
Bridges flow east.
Words arrive by night without knocking.

---

[11] There is a recording of Lehto and I reading this at PennSound <writing.upenn.edu/pennsound/x/Lehto.php>. I collected the poem in *Recalculating* (Chicago: University of Chicago Press, 2014), p. 29. The third version is Lehto's "barbaric" English translation in *Lake Onega and Other Poems* (Helsinki; ntamo), p. 19 and 143. See also Leevi Lehto, Frederik Hertzberg, Bernstein, "On The Origins, State, and Future Perspectives of Finno-Saxon" (2004), *The Conversant* (2012): <theconversant.org/?p=1759>.

Tämä tapahtui kaukaisessa maassa tässä lähellä.
Olen sanonut tästä jo monta kertaa.
Talon jokaisessa veeseessä on valo.
Sillat virtaavat itään.

Tamed tapestry's caressed master's tasseled luaus.
O when sanity tasted of muffled curtsy.
Talon — Jokasta's vivisected valor.
Silly virtual item.

This happened in a faraway country nearby.
I've said about this many times before.
In every toilet of the house there is a light on.
Bridges flow east.

Maaseudulla puut eivät vielä olleet lähteneet juoksuun.
Tämä tapahtui kaukaisessa maassa tässä lähellä.
Olen sanonut tästä jo monta kertaa.
Talon jokaisessa veeseessä on valo.

Medusa pouts as vat's veil's oldest lament jokes.
Tamed tapestry's caressed master's tasseled luaus.
O when sanity tasted of muffled curtsy.
Talon — Jokasta's vivisected valor.

In countryside the trees had not broken into run yet.
This happened in a faraway country nearby.
I've said about this many times before.
In every toilet of the house there is a light on.

Presidentti itse oli täysin lamaantunut.
Maaseudulla puut eivät vielä olleet lähteneet juoksuun.
Tämä tapahtui kaukaisessa maassa tässä lähellä.
Olen sanonut tästä jo monta kertaa:

President — he itsy, oily, tainted, laminated.
Medusa pouts as vat's veil's oldest lament jokes.
Tamed tapestry's caressed master's tasseled luaus.
O when sanity tasted of muffled curtsy.

The President himself was utterly paralysed.
In countryside the trees had not broken into run yet.
This happened in a faraway country nearby.
I've said about this many times before:

talon jokaisessa veeseessä on valo,
sillat virtaavat itään ja
sanat tulevat yöllä koputtamatta.

Talon — Jokasta's vivisected valor.
Silly virtual item, yah!
Sane as tugged vat, your love, kaput.

in every toilet of the house there is a light on,
bridges flow east, and
words arrive by night without knocking.

There is a kind of perverse pleasure in trying to create the same (*homo*)
from difference (*hetero*): homophonics is pataque(e)rical. The homophonic sublime is also the dream of a pure poetry, words for their own sake,
the cry of their occasion, "COME CI": *only this and nothing more.*[12]

A pure homophonic (or isophonic or synphonic) translation would
be the same words brought into a new language, not at all uncommon
for proper names and place names. The Mexican conceptualist Ulises Carrión plays on this possibility with his "The translation of 'Pedro
Páramo,'" a reference to the 1955 novel by Juan Rulfo:

---

[12] I reflect on these echoes of Mallarmé, Stevens, and Poe in "The Pataquerical Imagi-
nation: Midrashic Antinomianism and the Promise of Bent Studies" in *Pitch of Poetry*
(Chicago: University of Chicago Press, 2016).

to English: Pedro Páramo
to French: Pedro Páramo
to Italian: Pedro Páramo
to German: Pedro Páramo
to Portuguese: Pedro Páramo
to Dutch: Pedro Páramo[13]

Homophonic translation is parasitic: a parasite that may want to live symbiotically with its source or may wish to replace it, at least in becoming a new poem in its own right, autonomous, no longer dependent on the original but an original of its own.

In "The Use of Poetry," Basil Bunting writes about reading Persian, German, Italian, and Welsh poetry to a class that did not know those languages. He genially insists that the students would get as much out of hearing a foreign language poem as hearing one in their own language, since pronouncing a word is more important than knowing its meaning.[14] While Bunting's recitation of foreign language poems incomprehensible to his students was a quite serious endeavor, I see a connection with postwar American comedian Sid Caesar's "doubletalking"— deliriously funny live verbal improvisations that sound like Italian, German, and Japanese speech but are composed on the tongue with made-up strings of words.[15] Where Caesar gets laughs, Bunting gets poetry.

Bunting's insistence on sound over meaning is an extension of his framing of poetry in terms of music. Perhaps the most common experience related to Bunting's modest proposal is listening to an opera sung in a language you do not know and feeling you are missing nothing, indeed, preferring to hear the original to having the libretto sung, in

---

[13] Heriberto Yépez, "Ulises Carrión's Mexican Discontinuities," in *Ulises Carrión: Dear Reader. Don't Read*, ed. Guy Schraenen (Madrid: Museo Nacional Centro de Arte Reina Sofía, 2016), p. 51.

[14] Cited in "Artifice of Absorption" in my *A Poetics* (Cambridge: Harvard University Press, 1992), p. 58.

[15] Al Kelly and Prof. Irwin Cory, both older than Caesar, pioneered the style. Caesar's own doubletalking professor is related to Cory's shtick (doubletalking in the sense of intellectual gibberish not foreign language mimicry). In a different vain, Ruth Draper in "The Actress," from around 1916, leaps into Slavic doubletalk: <ruthdraper.com/selected-monologues/>.

11

translation, in your own language; and, moreover, preferring to listen without subtitles. It's no coincidence that opera parody is crucial to Caesar's doubletalking.

The *zaum* poems of Russian futurians Velimir Khlebnikov and Aleksei Kruchenykh were composed of synthesized or invented words that, whether intend or not, broke down the barriers of nationalist tongues and evoked species-wide listening, something that might be compared to Esperanto, despite the radical differences. "Incantation by Laughter" (1909) is the best-known zaum poem. My Khlebnikov transcreation follows the sound:

> We laugh with our laughter [O, rassmeites', smekhachi!]
> loke laffer un loafer [O, zasmeites', smekhachi]
> sloaf lafker int leffer [Chto smeyutsya smekhami]
> lopp lapter und loofer [chto smeyanstvuyut smeyal'no]
> loopse lapper ung lasler [O, zasmeites' usmeyal'no!]
> pleap loper ech lipler [O, rassmeshishch nadsmeyal'nykh]
> bloop uffer unk oddurk [smekh usmeinykh smekhachei!]
> floop flaffer ep flubber [O, issmeisya rassmeyal'no]
> fult lickles eng tlickers [smekh nadesmeinykh smeyachei!]
> ac laushing ag lauffing uk [Smeievo, smeievo,]
> luffing ip luppling uc [Usmei, osmei, smeshiki, smeshiki,]
> lippling ga sprickling [Smeyunchiki, smeyunchiki,]
> urp laughter oop laughing [O, rassmeites', smekhachi!]
> oop laughing urp laughter [O, zasmeites', smekhachi!]][16]

In modernist poetry, *zaum* is the most radical—and perhaps hysterical—extension of the sublime ideal of a poem being *only itself,* a cry of its occasion, "only this," overthrowing a subservience to representational meaning, or a parasitic relation to an original. Khlebnikov may have desired a deeper ur-Slavic but he also wrote of his desire for "a single human conversation"; in some sense— "beyonsense "— *zaum* echoes

---

[16] My American version was published in *Recalculating*, p. 94. I did a bilingual reading with Probstein, archived at PennSound with related recordings: <writing.upenn. edu/pennsound/x/Khlebnikov.php >.

international socialism.[17] On the Dada side, there are the sound poetry inventions at the Cabaret Voltaire, one hundred years ago, especially the work of Hugo Ball; and the ur-text of sound poetry, composed from 1922 to 1932, Kurt Schwitters's "Ursonate."[18]

Within American popular religious culture, there is speaking in tongues (glossolalia)—the spontaneous utterance, as if possessed, of an unintelligible or foreign language, which Jennifer Scappettone contrasts with xenoglossia.[19] Within American popular music, consider the scat singing of Ella Fitzgerald and Cab Calloway.

Reuven Tsur argues that you can't hear verbal utterances as non-verbal, but a poem can surely try to entice you by foregrounding the physical materiality of language, short-circuiting semantic processing.[20] Then

---

[17] *Zaum* is translated as both "trans-sense" and "beyond sense." According to Probstein, Khlebnikov "rejected borrowings from foreign languages and invented Russian words even for new scientific and technological phenomena. … Although Khlebnikov supported the October revolution, he was more concerned with the future unity of all humankind: 'Fly, human constellation, / Further on, further into space / And merge the Earth's tongues / Into a single human conversation.' … Both Khlebnikov and Kruchenykh spoke of *zaum* and 'the self-sufficient' word, but each interpreted those terms differently." Probstein quotes Khlebnikov on his search for "the magic touchstone of all Slavic words, … a self-sufficient language" that provides a path to the "universal language" of *zaum. — River of Time*, pp. 11, 15, 17.

[18] Listen to Schwitters, Ball, and the Russian futurians on PennSound <writing.upenn.edu/pennsound>.

[19] "Xenoglossia … refers to the intelligible use of a natural language one has not learned formally or does not know and is distinguishable from … glossolalia, or lexically incommunicative utterances. … Such tales of miraculous translation evince a yearning for the promise of correspondence between languages, and thereby of erased cultural difference." Jennifer Scappetone, "Phrasebook Pentecosts and Daggering Lingua Francas in the Poetry of LaTasha N. Nevada Diggs" in *The Fate of Difficulty in the Poetry of Our Time*, edited by Charles Altieri and Nicholas D. Nace (Evanston, IL: Northwestern University Press, 2018), p. 265.

[20] In *What Makes Sound Patterns Expressive? The Poetic Mode of Speech Perception* (Durham: Duke University Press, 1992), Reuven Tsur offers a groundwork for recognizing the expressivity of sound patterns, following Roman Jakobson's work on sound symbolism (sound iconicity). (Jakobson published a zaum collaboration with Kruchenykh in 1914 and wrote an essential account of Khlebnikov.) Tsur's cognitive poetics is immediately useful for literary sound studies. Born in 1932 in Transylvania, Tsur's native language is Hungarian. He started as a translator (into Hungarian

again, what's verbal and what's not is a matter of framing. We can hear a brook talking to us, can make animal sounds, and even turn the clackity-clacking of a sewing machine into a song.

The transformation of voicing or homophonically mimicking mechanical or machine sounds is its own genre of "sound-alike" poems. In Gertrude Stein's "If I Told Him: A Completed Portrait of Picasso" (1923), she echoes the sound of a shutter opening and closing: "Shutters shut and open so do queens. Shutters shut and shutters and so shutters shut and shutters and so and so shutters and so shutters shut and so shutters shut and shutters and so."[21] Then jump ahead to 2012 and Michael Winslow's mimicking the sound of 32 different historical typewriters.[22]

In Western poetry, birdsong has been a foundational metaphor for poetry, especially the nightingale's song. The earliest homophonic poetry would then be mimicry of birdsong in human language. Robert Grenier took this almost literally, writing a series of poems in 1975, *Sentences Toward Birds* that transcribed, into "the American," the "actual" sounds of birds in his immediate environment. Here are three of the poems, which, like his later *Sentences*, are each printed on individual cards:

why you say you see later

didn't see go to a

A BIRD / who would call / not for but for you / in the day[23]

---

and later Hebrew), getting his PhD at Sussex (UK). Now retired from Tel Aviv University, he still active in his research. He lives in Jerusalem. More Tsur at <www.tau.ac.il/~tsurxx>.

[21] Gertrude Stein, "If I Told Him: A Completed Portrait of Picasso": <writing.upenn.edu/pennsound/x/Stein/If-I-Told-Him.php>.

[22] "The History of the Typewriter Recited by Michael Winslow": <openculture.com/2014/06/the-history-of-the-typewriter.html>.

[23] Robert Grenier, *Sentences Toward Birds* (Kensington, CA: L Publications , 1975), online at <eclipsearchive.org/projects/BIRDS/birds.html>.

More recently, Hanna Tuulikki's "Air falbh leis na h-eòin—Away with the Birds" (2010 to 2015) has explored the "mimesis" of bird sounds in Gaelic poetry and song.[24]

In *aaaaw to zzzzd: The Word of Birds*, John Bevins not only provides a "lexicon" of birdsongs— "chinga, chinga, chinga" is the homophonic signature of the swamp sparrow-- but also a set of "mnemonics," such as the song sparrow's lyric refrain, "maids, maids, maids, put on your tea, kettle, kettle, kettle,"[25] which makes me burst into song, as if this is Broadway musical:

Maids, maids, maids
Put on your tea
Kettle, kettle, kettle.
No time to waste
Get out your bass
Fiddle, fiddle, fiddle.
Young lads make haste
Dance to your love's
Riddle, riddle, riddle.[26]

Bevins also suggests a motto for the homophonic sublime is his adaption of Walter Pater on music—"All art aspires to the condition of birdsong" (p. 15).

But perhaps the ultimate revenge of the long tradition of homophonics belongs to Sparkie Williams, "the talking budgie," a bird who, in the mid-1950s, was able to parrot a wide range of English words, mimicking human speech.[27]

A decade after Sparkie, Michael McClure's *Ghost Tantras* (1964) features a partially invented vocabulary that he calls "beast language" (guttural, expressive), which brings to mind a kind of primitive *zaum*

---

[24] Hanna Tuulikki, "Air falbh leis na h-eòin—Away with the Birds" and "Guth an eEòin" —"Voice of the Bird": <hannatuulikki.org/portfolio/awbirds> and <score.awaywiththebirds.co.uk>.

[25] John Bevins, *aaaaw to zzzzd: The Word of Birds* (Cambridge, MA: M.I.T. Press, 2010), pp. 48, 114. Bevins makes the argument for birdsong as music, comparing the experience to hearing songs in a foreign language (pp. 15-17) .

[26] A poem I based on the sound of the song sparrow.

[27] See Andrew Dodds, *I, Sparkie* (UK: Information as Material, 2013).

(McClure references Vladimir Mayakovsky). McClure wanted to find a level of language that invoked animality:

> Grahhr! Grahhhr! Ghrahhhrrr! Ghrahhr. Grahhrrr.
> Grahhr-grahhhhrr! Grahhr. Gahrahhrr Ghrahhhrrrr.
> Gharrrrr. Ghrahhr! Ghrarrrrr. Ghanrrr. Ghrahhhrr.
> Ghrahhrr. Ghrahr. Grahhr. Grahharrr. Grahhrr.
> Grahhhhr. Grahhhr. Gahar. Ghmhhr. Grahhr. Grahhr.
> Ghrahhr. Grahhhr. Grahhr. Gratharrr! Grahhr.
> Ghrahrr. Ghraaaaaaahrr. Grhar. Ghhrarrr! Grahhrr.
> Ghrahrr. Gharr! Ghrahhhhr. Grahhrr. Ghraherrr.

The 1964 and 1966 recordings he made reading his poems to lions are powerful poetic documents, notable for how much more expressive and poignant are the roars of the lions than are the homophonic translations of the poet, whose human language echoes wanly against the formidable sounds of the beasts.[28] Wittgenstein famously remarked, "Wenn ein Löwe sprechen könnte, wir könnten ihn nicht verstehen," a homosyntactical (word-for-word) translation is "If a Lion speak could, we could him not understand."[29] But when the lion roars, in a duet with McClure's mimicking, we hear the sound as song, a wail, perhaps a lament. The lion is growling at the human intruder's appropriation, as if to say I am the king of my own language, do not mock me. And growling at us, the unseen listeners: *beware*!

Listening to a poem or opera in a language foreign to you, but feeling you get it all the same, is a far cry from homophonic translation: it leaves the original just as is, the foreignizing occurring in the listener's response. If the aim of a poem is to foreground the materiality of sound,

---

[28] "Michael McClure Reads to Lions": <jacket2.org/commentary/michael-mcclure-reads-lions>.

[29] German text quoted, along with a discussion of Anscombe's translation of *Philosophical Investigations*, in Marjorie Perloff, *Wittgenstein's Ladder: Poetic Language and the Strangeness of the Ordinary* (Chicago: University of Chicago Press, 1996), pp. 74-75. See Ludwig Wittgenstein, *Philosophical Investigations*, tr. G.E.M. Anscombe, 2nd edition (Oxford: Blackwell, 1958), p. 223. The revised 4th edition of the translation by P. M. S. Hacker and Joachim Schulte (Blackwell, 2009) gives the line as "If a lion could talk, we wouldn't be able to understand it"; for Anscombe the lion is "him."

then listening to a language you don't know is a kind of poetic experience. But that only goes so far. Listening to a poem in language you don't know gets less interesting the longer it goes on; entropy sets in faster than a mosquito dodging a fly swatter. Sid Caesar's doubletalk is hilarious because it is exaggerated in its stereotyping and because you know he is going on nerve: it's a high-wire act and the wire is not that long. In contrast, homophonic translation allows for extensions and textual subtly since it goes beyond imitation into commentary and because it is able to create a new poem in the new language.

2. Wot We Wukkerz Want

Let me to make a brief detour in my account to consider Edgar Allan Poe's "The Philosophy of Literary Composition," published in 1846, near the end of the troubled poet's life. Poe's delightfully bizarre paean to artifice is, in part, a send-up of spontaneously inspired, frenzied, sincere verse, what Poe calls "ecstatic intuition." Writing about "The Raven," Poe claims that the origin of a poem is a set of logically predetermined effects, including sound effects: meaning comes after. In effect, Poe attempts to treat verbal composition as if it were musical composition. Poe's elaborate and impossible rules for poetic composition bring to mind Sid Caesar's grifter-like elaboration of impossible rules for a card game in his early 1950s sketch "The Poker Game."[30] Both Poe and Caesar offer a kind of doubletalk, or talking out of both sides of the mouth, though, in these cases, not deceptively, since their discourse foregrounds the absurdity, even though performed with straight faces. In the comic pathos of Poe's insistence on the author's total control of the poem through the rigidly pre-determined, Poe never breaks character, that of the author whose sole aim is beauty, achieved by maximizing melancholy (not to say pathos). Poe elaborates his doubletalk with absolute conviction. Like Caesar, Poe aimed to please "the popular and the critical taste."

Both Baudelaire's and Mallarmé's translations of "The Raven" (1865 and 1875, respectively) swerve toward the homophonic, often echoing Poe's exact sound patterns.[31] Even if you don't know French, you'd

---

[30] Sid Caesar, "The Poker Game," *Your Show of Shows* (date unknown): <youtu.be/RyNSFLkXTvA> .

[31] See Robin Seguy's 2015 hypertext presentations of the translations at <text-works.org>.

recognize "The Raven" if the translations were performed. A performed Yiddish translation by I. Kissen is always already a homophonic translation.[32] "The Raven" is as identifiable as Beethoven's Fifth, and if you don't know Yiddish, it can seem as if it is doubletalk.

The modern history of radical translation in American poetry might reasonably begin with Pound's Chinese adaptions but I want now to briefly cite his two translations of Guido Cavalcanti (1250-1300), "Donna mi prega," the first from 1928, the second from 1934. Pound gives the constraints, worthy of Poe's "Philosophy of Composition" or Caesar's poker rules: "Each strophe is articulated by 14 terminal and 12 inner rhyme sounds, which means that 52 of every 154 syllables are bound into pattern."[33]

> Because a lady asks me, I would tell
> Of an affect that comes often and is fell
> And is so overweening: Love by name.
> E'en its deniers can now hear the truth. (1928, *Pound's Cavalcanti*, 171)
>
> •
>
> A lady asks me
>   I speak in season
> She seeks reason for an affect, wild often
> That is so proud he hath Love for a name
> Who denys it can hear the truth now (1934, *Pound's Cavalcanti*, 179)

---

[32] I. Kissen's Yiddish, "The Raven: Multilingual," cut 21: <archive.org/details/raven_multilingual_0903>.

[33] *Pound's Cavalcanti*, p. 216. Pounds' commentary on "Donna mi prega" appeared in *The Dial* (with the subtitle "Medievalism") in 1928; this article included his translation in its first publication; a few years later it was collected in *Make It New*. See my related discussion in "Objectivist Blues," *Attack of the Difficult Poems* (Chicago: University of Chicago Press, 2011) pp. 135-36. Nathan Kageyama reverses the dynamic in his translation of Pound's "The Return" into Hawaiian pidgin in *Tinfish* 3 (1996): <writing.upenn.edu/epc/ezines/tinfish>: "See, they return; ah, see the tentative / Movements, and the slow feet, / The trouble in the pace and the uncertain / Wavering!" becomes "Spock em, dey stay come; auwe, spock da scayed / Movaments, an' da luau feet, / Stay all twis' an' kooked / Walkin' all jag!"

In 1940, at the beginning of World War II, Louis Zukofsky took the Cavalcanti translations to another dimension. What he produced was not a homophonic translation but rather a sound transcreation that radically accented the poem, making it, in part, an ethnic dialect poem, a sort of Yiddish doubletalking, where doubletalking implies bilingualism and double consciousness.[34] As with his inaugural "Poem Beginning 'The,'" Zukofsky radically engaged an American vernacular, following the model of Pound and Williams, and he brought it home, to a *mamaloshen* (mother tongue), homey and homely, but with a majestic beauty brought over from the sound structure of the Cavalcanti:

> A foin lass bodders me I gotta tell her
> Of a fact surely, so unrurly, often'
> 'r 't comes 'tcan't soften its proud neck's called love mm ...[35]

Perhaps the closest recent work of this kind—a translation into a marked, comic dialect, with accent über alles— is the riotous "The Kommunist Manifesto or Wot We Wukkerz Want"—"Redacted un traduced intuht' dialect uht' west riding er Yorkshuh bi Steve McCaffery, eh son of that shire" in 1977.[36]

---

[34] The most likely Yiddish word for doubletalk is פֿאָנפֿען (*fonfen*)— mumbling. In contrast to Jeffrey Shandler's term "postvernacular" in *Adventures in Yiddishland* (Berkeley: University of California Press, 2006), pp. 19-27, I'd call this work *patavernacular*.

[35] In 1940, Zukofsky privately circulated "A foin lass" in *FIRST HALF of "A"- 9*, a numbered and autographed edition of 55. Zukofsky included sources for "*A*"-9, including "Donna mi priegha [sic]," 22 pages on value and commodification excerpted from Marx's *Capital* and *Value Price and Profit*, a short excerpt from Stanley Allen's *Electronics and Waves: A Short Introduction to Atomic Physics* (1932), "translations of Cavalcanti's Canzone" by Pound (both versions) and vernacular versions by Jerry Reisman and Zukofsky, followed by a note on the form and "*A*"-9, first half, and concluding with a two-page "Restatement" of the poem. The first publication of "A foin lass" was in Zukofsky's *Selected Poems*, which I edited (New York: Library of America American Poets Project, 2006), p. 152. You can hear my performance of the poem at <writing.upenn.edu/ezurl/5/> and Zukofsky's performance at <writing.upenn.edu/ezurl/6/>: Zukofsky performs it with a high, formal tone, neutralizing accent, while I emphasize a Yiddish/Brooklyn twang, performing a kind of "Jewface." I discuss "Jewface" in "Objectivist Blues" in *Attack of the Difficult Poems*, p. 142. (I heard Zukofsky's performance only after I had made my recording.)

[36] Steve McCaffery, "Kommunist Manifesto": <writing.upenn.edu/library/

3. Doubletalk

Discussion of homophonic translation is generally placed in the context of radical poetic innovation. I want to contrast that lineage with two examples from popular culture, one from the postwar American comic Sid Caesar and the other from *Benny Lava*, a recent viral YouTube video. Doubletalk, as Caesar uses the term, is homophonic translation of a foreign-language movie, opera scenario, or everyday speech into an improvised performance that mimics the sound of the source language with made-up, *zaum*-like invented vocabulary. Consider an uproarious 2015 performance by French poet Joseph Gugliemi, where he performs a made-up language under the guise of reading a poetry text, which at one point he shows to be all blank pages.[37] In contrast, literary homophonic translation begins with a defined foreign-language poem as source text and creates a new work in English that mimics the sound of the original.

The best example of Caesar's "double-talk" is a concert in which he moves through four languages, starting with French and moving to German and Italian, ending with Japanese (replete with recognizable anchor words, such an Mitsubishi, Datsun and sushi.)[38] Taken as a whole, this

---

McCaffey-Steve_Kommunist-Manifesto.html>. McCaffery and Jed Rasula edited a crucial anthology of sound writing and invented vocabularies called *Imagining Language* (Cambridge, MA: M.I.T. Press, 1998). "Sound writing" echoes "sound poetry" and what Richard Kostelanetz anthologized as *Text–Sound Texts* (New York: William Morrow, 1980).

[37] Performance by Joseph Guglielmi in the Paris studio of Anne Slacik on Oct. 11, 2015:
<writing.upenn.edu/pennsound/x/deformance.php>.

[38] "Sid Caesar Performing in Four Different Languages": <writing.upenn.edu/ezurl/7>, date unknown. See also: "Sid Caesar Double-Talk Routine" (interview) <youtu.be/ iL7efWcaVnk>; "Sid Caesar, Le Grande Amour" <youtu.be/JGHih5ISPhQ>, French doubletalk film satire; "Sid Caesar, The Russian Arthur Godfrey" <youtu.be/FHbscd-j7OtU>, Russian doubletalk, ending with Carl Reiner doing movie star impressions in Russian doubletalk; and "Sid Caesar: Der Flying Ace" <youtu.be/GhXRZ7yw7Nw>. Caesar discusses "double-talk" in Sid Caesar with Eddy Friedfeld, *Caesar's Hours: My Life in Comedy, with Love and Laughter* (New York: Public Affairs, 2003), p. 58. "Sid Caesar's 80th Birthday Party" features a tour-de-force reprise, with Caesar, reading notes, double-talking in French, German, Spanish, Italian, and Japanese <youtu.be/FETaKPtdaJM>.

five-minute performance is macaronic— a burlesque jumble or comic hodgepodge of different languages. The camera pans to the audience during each segment to show benign and approving laughter. The serial movement from language to language also suggests a nomadic display of multi-lingual code-switching. It brings ... home ... the final line of Charles Reznikoff's 1934 poem about diaspora:

> and God looked and saw the Hebrews
> citizens of the great cities,
> talking Hebrew in every language under the sun.[39]

Though perhaps this might be revised to say Yiddish rather than Hebrew, follow Ariel Resnikoff's discussion of the pervasiveness of Yiddish in Jewish culture.[40]

The first archival footage we have of Caesar's mimicry is from *Tars and Spars*, a Coast Guard-produced war movie from 1946 in which the 24-year-old Caesar does "Wings over Bominshissel," his "airplane-movie number," written with his brother Dave and created the year before for a "tabloid musical" recruitment revue for the Spars (the Coast Guard Women's Reserve). [41] The show was written by Howard Dietz (who wrote the lyrics for "Dancing in the Dark" and "Alone Together") and Vernon Duke (born in 1903 as Vladimir Dukelsky, who wrote the music of "April in Paris" and "Taking a Chance on Love").[42] Sid was billed as "Sydney Caesar." The first bit of Caesar's multicultural "double-talk languages" is part of the ludicrous "I Love Eggs" number, where after doing

---

[39] Charles Reznikoff, "Joshua at Shechem," *Jerusalem the Golden* in *Complete Poems*, vol. 1 (Santa Barbara, CA: Black Sparrow Press, 1976), p. 126.

[40] Ariel Resnikoff, "Home Tongue Earthquake: The Radical Afterlives of Yiddishland," PhD Dissertation, University of Pennsylvania, 2019.

[41] *Tars and Spars* (1946): <youtu.be/0HdD25USDV0> (among other places). Caesar's Russian doubletalk begins around 48 minutes; his airplane routine begins at around 69 minutes. Caesar discusses the routine in *Caesar's Hours*, pp. 54-58.

[42] In addition to being a composer, Dukelsky, who to some extent discovered (and surely offered great support to) a very young Caesar, was a futurist-influenced Russian poet as well as translator of Frost, Stevens, cummings, and Pound. Perhaps he is the "missing link" between Caesar and modernist poetry. See Elena Dubrovina, "'The Song of Time': Vladimir Dukelsky, Poet and Composer <gostinaya.net/?p=12060>.

a Mexican hat dance and playing a German cook, Caesar dives into a fake Russian song lyric, "Eggs Romanoff," after singing a few parodic verses in English set to what sounds like, that is to say, anticipates, the Russian folk song pastiche "To Life" from the 1964 musical *Fiddler on the Roof.*

In a video interview, Caesar says he didn't do mimicry but sound effects, an airplane taking off or the rain.[43] I take this to mean he viewed his foreign language and foreign accent mimicry as an extension of imitating mechanical or natural sounds. Indeed, in the movie he does *voices* and gestures and faces and pantomimed actions, moving from one to another to another as part of a rapid fire collage of schticks, seguing from the sound of a plane taking off to the barked command of a pompous British military officer, with tones of Churchill (from some barked words Caesar moves in a low grumble— gewd luck my boyyyy, grrr, awwww— with no discernable words, a kind of proto sound poem). In the bit, Caesar notes how the American planes sound mellifluous while the Nazi planes sound ominous. He segues from the sound of a Nazi airplane motor right into German-Nazi doubletalk, together with a full sound opera of a machine gun battle between the two planes, followed by aerial bombardment of German targets. "I did all the sound effects with my mouth, including the starting of the airplane engines and the throttle" (*Caesar's Hours*, 54).

Caesar was the most important and influential comedy star of early American television, a key member of a generation that included Lenny Bruce (born Leonard Schneider in 1925), Jackie Gleason (born 1916), Ernie Kovacs (born 1919), and Jerry Lewis (born Joseph [or Jerome] Levitch in 1926). Isaac Sidney "Sid" Caesar was born in 1922 and died in 2014. His parents were Jewish immigrants, his father was from Poland and mother from Russia, both coming to New York as children, which means that Yiddish would have been their home language.

Yiddish is a nomadic language, not based in any nation but creating a common tongue for diasporic Jews in Poland, Hungary, Russia, and America, among other places. While sometimes thought to be a dialect

---

[43] "Sid Caesar Interview, part 2," with Dan Pasternack, March 14, 1997, Archive of American Television: <emmytvlegends.org/interviews/people/sid-caesar>.

of German, Yiddish is its own language, spoken by people who did not necessarily know German. As a consequence of the Systematic Extermination of the European Jews, compounded by Israel's turn against Yiddish by selecting Hebrew as its national language, Yiddish came to be a dead language, like Latin, though it persists, with vitality, in pockets.

In *Bridges of Words: Esperanto and the Dream of a Universal Language*, Esther Schor tells the story the invention of Esperanto by L. L. Zamenhof (1859-1917), an Eastern European Jew who grew up speaking Russian at home, Polish and German for business, Yiddish with other Jews, and Hebrew in synagogue. Zamenhof said that the hostility of one group of language speakers to another "made me feel that men did not exist, only Russians, Poles, Germans, Jews, and so on."[44] He conceived Esperanto as a way to overcome ethnic and national barriers, which echoes, while departing from, Khlebnikov's "single human conversation" (and given *zaum*'s "magical" derivations from Russian root words). Prior to his 1887 manifesto for Esperanto, Zamenhof had gone through a proto-Zionist period, where he advocated a Latin-scripted Yiddish. His vision for Esperanto's universality, in contrast, pushed back against anti-Semitic projections of a secret Jewish language. Then again in 1901, Zamenhof proposed Esperanto for an ethically (rather than ethnically) based Jewish language, an alternative to the liturgical Hebrew and the polyglot ("jargonized") Yiddish.

"Instead of being absorbed by the Christian world, we [Jews] shall absorb them," Zamenhof proclaimed in 1907 (pp. 82, 132). Schor comments that, in this context, Judaize means not to turn into Jews but to make justice and fraternity our foundation.

Sid Caesar was not likely to have known of Zamenhof or Esperanto. As a teenager, Caesar was a musician and comedian, if not quite sociable enough to be a *tummler* (MC/comic/entertainer-in-chief), in the Borscht Belt (the Jewish resort area in the Catskill mountains, just outside New York), where he absorbed classic burlesque sketch comedy (*Caesar's Hours*, 34). In 1942, he enlisted in the Coast Guard, where he ended up doing musical reviews. In 1948, live TV called, first through the invitation

---

[44] Esther Schor, *Bridges of Words: Esperanto and the Dream of a Universal Language*, (New York: Henry Holt, 2016), pp. 63.

of Milton Berle. Caesar got in on the ground floor of the new medium. He was the star of the *Admiral Broadway Revue* in 1949. In 1950-1954 he starred in *Your Show of Shows*, the most watched television show of the time. He continued to do weekly TV from New York till 1958. In these shows, everything was performed live—though a team of comedy writers, including Mel Brooks, Woody Allen, Carl Reiner, and Neil Simon, wrote the sketches. But there were no cue cards or teleprompters.

In his autobiography, Caesar tells a story that brings Zamenhof to mind (and ear). At his father's restaurant, where he worked, speakers of different language groups sat at different tables and Caesar would go from table to table mimicking the sounds of the customer's native tongues, much to their delight. The scene recalls lines by Hebrew poet Avot Yeshurun (born 1904) addressed to his mother, in which the poet expresses his sense of the loss of Yiddish, his mother/other tongue, while evoking a primal experience of doubletalk: "You who hear a language in seventy translations / at night in the garden of Dizengoff Square."[45]

> My love of music ... led me to appreciate the melodies and rhymes of foreign language. I learned my signature double-talk, which was a fast-paced blend of different sounds and weds mimicking [different languages] from the customers at my father's restaurant. (*Caesar's Hours*, 15)

Key to Caesar's homophonic genius is that he was a professional jazz saxophone player before he became a comedian. The way some musicians can learn a song or a symphony by ear, Caesar learned languages, as if they were musical scores. One of his classic sketches involves his

---

[45] Avot Yeshurun, "Got fun Avrohom," *Kapella Kolot* (Tel Aviv: Siman Keriyah, 1977). Quoted by Neta Stahl in a review of Naomi Brenner's *Lingering Bilingualism: Modern Hebrew and Yiddish Literatures in Contact* in *Comparative Literature* 69:3 (2017), p. 350. The title of the poem means "God of Abraham" and refers to a Yiddish prayer for women (mothers), to protect Israel from harm; Dizengoff Square is in Tel Aviv. For homophonic plays between Hebrew and Yiddish see Roy Greenwald, "Homophony in Multiligual Jewish Cultures," *Dibur* 1 (2016): <arcade.stanford.edu/dibur/homophony-multilin-gual-jewish-cultures≥ (Greenwald discusses Yeshurun). I am grateful to Ariel Resnikoff for discussions about Yeshurun. See his essay, "Louis Zukofsky and Mikhl Likht, 'A Test of Jewish American Modernist Poetics'" in *Jacket2* (2013): <jacket2.org/commentary/ariel-res-nikoff-louis-zukofsky-and-mikhl-likht-test-jewish-american-modernist-poetics-p-0>.

miming a pianist playing Grieg's *Piano Concerto in A Minor*. The music was being played offstage, but for all the world you'd think Caesar was playing it, hitting the notes *en plein air*, as if sound and gesture were totally indivisible. Think of Jerry Lewis's classic conducting sketch in *The Bellboy* (1960) or his Count Basie mime in *The Errand Boy* (1961). Caesar puts his gift for the homophonic succinctly: "To me it's song."[46]

Caesar's most famous opera sketch is "Gallipacci," a 1955 parody of *Pagliacci*.[47] Caesar, in the perfect role of the clown, sings in doubletalk Italian, mixed with some English, which allows him to cue plot points and adds a comic effect. His first number is, in effect, a homophonic version of Leoncavallo's libretto sung to an *operaschmerz* pastiche of Leoncavallo's score (doubletalk music). But Caesar's next bit is an Italian doubletalk version of "Just One of Those Things," a 1935 Cole Porter song (with a whiff of Leoncavallo to boot), presented to resemble one of the most poignant scenes in Italian opera. Indeed, the whole cast sings (and speaks) in Italian doubletalk, occasionally mixed with stereotypical versions of ethnic Italian-American speech. At one point Nanette Fabray sings (in Italian doubletalk à la Leoncavallo) the Fanny Brice standard, "My Man"; later Fabray and Carl Reiner throw in "Take Me Out to the Ball Game." The chorus opens with an Italian doubletalk operatic version of "Santa Claus (*Gallipacci*) is Coming to Town." The rousing final scene, the clown's tragic song after killing his wife, is set to the tune of "The Yellow Rose of Texas," with the cast singing in Italian doubletalk.

Caesar's doubletalk shtick was often used in elaborate parodies of foreign movies.[48] The best known is his version of Vittorio de Sica's 1948

---

[46] Transcript, CNN: Larry King Live, "Hail Sid Caesar," Sept. 7, 2001 <transcripts.cnn.com/TRANSCRIPTS/0109/07/lkl.00.html>.

[47] "Sid Caesar, Gallipacci," *Caesar's Hour*, Oct. 10, 1955. The cast included Nanette Fabray, Reiner, and Howard Morris: <youtu.be/5OW7GoIl0T8>. The sketch was revived, in a watered-down version that undercuts the operatic doubletalk, on *The Sid Caesar, Imogene Coca, Carl Reiner, Howard Morris Reunion Special*, April 4, 1967 <http://youtu.be/ScqZW2NQwPY>.

[48] Reiner takes the credit for suggesting the foreign film parodies, noting that he could also do "double talk" and sold the idea to Caesar by laying it on him. See his interview in *They'll Never Put that on the Air: An Oral History of Taboo-breaking TV Comedy* by Allan Neuwirth (New York: Allsworth Press, 2006), pp. 5-6. Reiner gives a slightly different account in *Where Have I Been: An Autobiography* by Sid Caesar with Bill

neorealist film, *Ladri di biciclette* (*The Bicycle Thief*), which focused on the difficult life in Italy immediately following the war. Caesar and company would go to see foreign films at Museum of Modern Art. "We did movies in Italian, French, German, and Japanese double-talk. We never wrote double-talk out word for word, just laid out the goals, the comic direction," he says in *Caesar's Hours* (212).

"I've always considered doubletalk [sic] to be a form of music ... with each language having its own rhythm," (*Caesar's Hours*, 211). For Caesar, the key to homophonic mimicry is "Lip movements and intonation" (*Caesar's Hours*, 15). At the Yonkers's 24-hour buffet and luncheonette, where he worked as a kid, the factory workers from Otis Elevator and other nearby factories and offices laughed heartily at his fluent ear: each table had a different language group and he moved from table to table, a multilectal collage epic poem in real time and space. Like Louis Zukofsky, though a generation younger, Caesar knew only Yiddish and English. But he realized his homophonic gift made people laugh.

> Nearly all [the customers] were young, single immigrants
> who would segregate into groups speaking Italian, Russian,
> Hungarian, Polish, French, Spanish, Lithuanian, and even
> Bulgarian. I would go from table to table, listening to the
> sounds. I learned how to mimic them, sounding as if I were
> actually speaking their language. They weren't offended.[49]

In Yonkers in the 1930s, such parody was viewed as welcoming, not offensive. Difference was what was common in his father's restaurant. To bend Rimbaud, *Everyone is an other.*

> I would even do double-talk in synagogue. I wasn't doing
> it disrespectfully, but out of a desire to fit in and impress.
> There seemed to be a race to finish the prayers among the
> synagogue elders, which would end with the winner closing

Davidson (New York: Crown Publishers, 1982), p. 109, which is the first and better of Caesar's two autobiographies, with its harrowing tale. In Adam Bernstein's Washington *Post* obituary for Reiner, Mel Brooks says, "Nobody could do *foreign gibberish* better than Sid Caesar, but this Reiner guy could keep up with him" (July 1, 2020, p. a10; italics added).

[49] *Where Have I Been*, p. 13. Caesar says that he was wanted to find a comedy that, unlike slapstick, did not "degrade another human being" (p. 30).

the prayer book shut while holding it up in the air. The double-talk made it seem like I was moving through the prayer book like a Torah scholar, as I would also slam the prayer book shut. The synagogue elders were in awe over my apparent expertise in the Scripture. (*Caesar's Hours*, 17)

The saying of Hebrew prayers quickly is often a matter of gesture and intonation, this is at the heart of davening, in which, like a Buddhist mantra, the sound carries the spirit. Indeed, for generations American Jews have learned to pronounce Hebrew without knowing what it means, something suggested by Zukofsky's homophonic translation of the Hebrew of *Job* in "*A*"-15.

In *Where Have I Been*, Caesar gives another origin story for his homophonic practice. It seems baby Sid didn't start to talk till he was 4, but he was already writing (40-41): "I'd sit at a table … for hours and make marks that *looked* exactly like writing. … It was like the beginning of the foreign-language double-talk I did later at the luncheonette." So there, Truman Capote!

Caesar's first cited (but not recorded) use of doubletalk was from *Six On, Twelve Off*, a Coast Guard review that he did with Vernon Duke in 1944 (*Where Have I Been*, 50-51). The doubletalk was part of a routine called "Conversation between Hitler and Donald Duck"— Caesar did both parts. The bit was likely inspired by the 1943 Walt Disney / RKO propaganda cartoon *Der Fuehrer's Face*, directed by Jack Kinney and originally titled *Donald Duck in Nutzi Land*, which won the Academy Award for Best Animated Short Film, though it was subsequently suppressed for fifty years. This sidesplitting short features the song Spike Jones made famous in 1942, "Der Fuehrer's Face," which was written by Oliver Wallace. *Donald Duck in Nutzi Land* bears a resemblance to *Ducktators*, directed by Norman McCabe (WB / Looney Tunes, 1942) as well as to *Daffy Duck—the Commando*, directed by Fritz Freleng (WB / Looney Tunes, 1943). *Daffy- the Commando* features snippets of parodic Nazi-inflected doubletalk and ends with Hitler giving a doubletalk speech (that is, a homophonic version of Hitler oratory), which is stopped by Donald hitting him with a giant mallet after which Hitler stutters and screams.[50]

---

[50] See Marc Shell's discussion of these cartoons, as well as *The Great Dictator* (and, at least in citation, *Modern Times*) in terms of the macaronic, in *Talking the Walk &*

But before Caesar or Looney Tunes did their German doubletalk, there was Charlie Chaplin's extended homophonic translation of a Hitler speech in *The Great Dictator* from 1940: doubletalk salted with English words. That speech is given by the dictator Adenoid Hynkel, whose double is Schultz, the Jewish barber. The film ends with a double of this speech, spoken by Schultz as Hynkel/Hitler. This rousing speech against tyranny, intolerance, and "national barriers," spoken in plain English and broadcast to the world, breaks the dictator's nightmarish spell. We can be sure Caesar, who idolized Chaplin, heard it. Just as he would have known Chaplin's Italian doubletalking "nonsense" song in *Modern Times* (1936):

> Se bella giu satore
> Je notre so cafore
> Je notre si cavore
> Je la tu la ti la twah[51]

Homophonic works are usually funny, if not outright comic. They succeed because they have a sense of humor about the apparent absurdity of the idea. It's the humor, and the sense of identification with the other, that inflects the homophonics of Zukofsky and Caesar, both of who grew up in a Yiddish-speaking household but for whom English was, if not the mother tongue, than the father tongue, the language they mastered. Ironically, for Caesar, doubletalk was not deceptive or artificial but a honing/homing into the language-spring of *mamaloshen*. Indeed, Caesar notes that some of his first jokes were based on translinguistic puns and mishearing between Yiddish and English, which greatly amused his audience, who were making their way to being American by moving from Yiddish to English. Caesar credits Yiddish dialect performers as precursors. He mentions Willie Howard, who sang Yiddish words to Mexican-themed skits (*Caesar's Hours*, 16). Fanny Brice comes to mind.

Walking the Talk: A Rhetoric of Rhythm (New York: Fordham University Press, 2015).

[51] "Nonsense Song from Modern Times": <charliechaplin.com/en/lyrics/articles/114-Song-from-Modern-Times-Titine>.

Caesar's approach to all his performance art is that it "had to have a basis in reality. It had to be believable" (*Caesar's Hours*, xxi). It is this believability—what Zukofsky called "sincerity"— that undercuts parody and irony: it allows language to be reinhabited ("objectification" in Zukofsky's sense) rather than mocked.[52] This, in turn, connects to Zukofsky's "An Foin Lass"—a translation that brings home the Cavalcanti, *makes it home* and a little bit homely. The doubleness in doubletalk is, then, not deception or evasion but double consciousness in W. E. B. Du Bois's sense—the consciousness of the dominant English but the echo of the *mamaloshen*. It's not about a return to an authentic original language, it's the dialectial relation of the two, the echopoetics, that is the ground. Doubletalk that foregrounds doubletalking as its own kind of poetry or verbal acrobatics. And just to bring this point ever more homeward: Caesar would intersperse Yiddish and English words into his doubletalk routines. As he boasts, a Yiddish word pronounced the right way can sound Japanese (*Caesar's Hours*, 214).

While all Caesar's doubletalk is done with good humor, his signature German doubletalk is also in effect proto-Nazi doubletalk and is laced with gentle, but devastating, mocking. The prime example is one of Caesar's best-known doubletalk skits, "The German General" from 1954, written with Mel Brooks.[53] With Howard Morris and Caesar both doing doubletalk, "The German General" is set in pre-war Germany. The first of two scenes focuses on what appears to be the elaborate dressing of a patrician general (Caesar) by his servile underling, who polishes his chest medals and puffs his gold braids. The second scene involves a radical reversal, turning satire into pathos: the General walks from the dressing room through a hotel lobby filled with swankily dressed people. He heads to the hotel entrance, where we realize he is the doorman, his military dress is just a fancy uniform. By detourning the proto-Nazi figure, the entirely doubletalked performance explodes the master-slave

---

[52] Louis Zukofsky, "Sincerity and Objectification with Special Reference to the Work of Charles Reznikoff," in *Prepositions +: The Collected Critical Essays*, ed. Mark Scroggins (Middletown, CT: Wesleyan University Press, 2000).

[53] "Sid Caesar, The German General": <youtu.be/5m6Czgl1acU>, broadcast on *Caesar's Hour*, Sept. 26, 1954. Caesar discusses the skit in *Caesar's Hours*, pp. 215-216. Mel Brooks takes the writing credit in a memorial tribute to Caesar on *Conan*, "Mel Brooks on Sid Caesar's Masterful Gibberish," Feb. 19, 2014: <youtu.be/RUHemC_dvuU>.

dialectic— not by switching roles but by undermining mastery through recontextualization (a change of frame in Erving Goffman's sense). The Jewish parasites, in Nazi eyes, inhabit and make their own the German language. With their double voicing, Caesar and Brooks are tricksters, signifying on the German. The sketch is based on two foreign-language films unlikely to have been seen by most of the mass audience of the TV show: F. W. Murnau's 1925 *The Last Laugh* and Jean Renoir's 1937 *Grand Illusion* (with Walt Disney's 1937 *Snow White and the Seven Dwarfs* thrown in for good measure). This combination of high and low culture was an intentional part of Caesar's method. The method required that the skits would work even if the audience didn't know the sources of the parody. The performances had to be works in their own right, much as it is the goal of homophonic translations for autonomy from the source, free of secondary (or parasitic) status— not by reversing the power dynamic but reframing it. Brooks would come back to this theme 13 years later with *The Producers*.[54]

Caesar's doubletalk uses the full prosodic resources of verbal language, foregrounding intonation, gesture, rhythm, syntax, and sound patterning rather than lexical identification. Doubletalk resembles sound poetry, but it is tied to the specific sounds and rhythms of the language being parodied. It is homophonic translation not of specific text but, rather, of the texture of the source language.

Like doubletalk, homophonic translation, *zaum,* sound poetry, and scat singing are not against expression; they are hyper-communicative. Sound writing makes meaning by other means (*kio signifas per aliaj rimedoj* in Esperanto); other, that is, than lexical. This is meaning for those who feel at home in the world, or want to make the world more homely (*gemütlich, haimish*). "At home," according to theologian Ernst Fuchs, "one does not speak so that people will understand but because people understand."[55] Language at home is marked by the temporal,

---

[54] Brooks wanted Caesar to play the part of the Nazi in the 1968 movie, but the studio nixed the idea (*Where Have I Been?*, p. 189).

[55] Ernst Fuchs, "The New Testament and the Hermeneutical Problem," in *New Frontiers in Theology*, vol. 2, *The New Hermeneutic*, tr. and ed. by James M. Robinson and John B. Cobb (New York: Harper and Row, 1964), p. 124 (italics removed). This quote, unsourced, comprises the 11th section of my "Three or Four Things I Know about

transient, always in-process "presence of a dialect": "Here language is emotional. Its understanding of time ranges between song and shout" (p. 126).

The presence of the word, that is, *verbing the word*, is antinomian: *the performance of language supersedes the law of language.*

> Only that which can become present as language is real. "For where meaning is, there also is language. And where language is, there is reality. Language belongs so closely to reality that it sets reality free for the first time: language ex-presses reality. …The word not merely conveys the concrete situation but creates it."[56]

In 1912, Franz Kafka gave an "Introductory Lecture on Jargon," a talk on Yiddish that he wrote as a prologue to a performance of Yiddish poetry. Yiddish represented for Kafka a "kind of immediacy of expression" in sharp contrast to the "endemic alienation of Western assimilated Jews" like himself.[57] Yiddish, for Kafka, is related to Fuchs's idea of a language of home. At the same time, Kafka saw Yiddish as *mißachtete*, a disregarded and stigmatized dialect, a language appropriated from other language, and a subculture argot (a "minor language" as Gilles Deleuze and Felix Guattari have it in *Kafka: Toward a Minor Literature*).

> [Yiddish] consists solely of foreign words. But these words are not firmly rooted in it, they retain the speed and liveliness with which they were adopted. Great migrations move through Yiddish, from one end to the other. All this German, Hebrew, French, English, Slavonic, Dutch, Rumanian, and even Latin, is seized with curiosity and frivolity once it is contained within Yiddish, and it

---

Him," *Content's Dream: Essays 1975-1985* (Los Angeles: Sun and Moon Press, 1985), p. 30. Fuchs's first name is incorrectly cited as "Eduard."

[56] Gerald G. O'Collins, "Reality as Language: Ernst Fuchs's Theology of Revelation," *Theological Studies*, 28:1 (Feb. 1967), pp. 77-78. In internal quote, O'Collins translates Fuchs.

[57] Richard T. Gray, Ruth V. Gross, Rolf J. Goebel, and Clayton Koelb, *A Franz Kafka Encyclopedia* (Westport, CT: Greenwood Press, 2005), p. 235. Eugene Ostashevsky pointed me to Kafka's talk.

takes a good deal of strength to hold all these languages together in this state.... It is only thieves' cant [Gaunersprache, Klezmer-loshen, argot] ... because Yiddish was, after all, for a long time a despised [mißachtete] language. ... And now the dialects enter into language's fabric of arbitration and law. Indeed, Yiddish as a whole consists only of dialect, even the written language [Schriftsprache, written speech] ... .[58]

Doubletalk is a kind of talk poem, to use David Antin's term; as with jazz, the performance is live and improvised; both of these elements are essential. Caesar's doubletalk, while markedly American, is accessible to those who don't know English, and in that sense, it works like *zaum*, sound poetry, and scat singing: verbal works that do not require knowledge of a specific national language (call it *transnational*, to give that term a different spin). During, and in the immediate wake of, the systematic extermination of the European Jews, Caesar's doubletalk broke down the barrier of national languages by creating a sense of the delightful *comradery of difference* and by diffusing ethnic tension. Difference is elided through immediate accessibility. The Groucho Marxian comedy of puns and verbal wit may be difficult for non-native speakers to fully understand; not so doubletalk. Doubletalk is verbal pantomime, as paradoxical as that sounds (or doesn't sound). It is words sublimed to music. In contrast, the American homophonic poem may have aspired to be non-English-bound but its reliance on puns and allusions may sometimes run counter to this.

Caesar's homophonics are all about accent and accent is always a matter of class and ethnicity. In American culture, to have a marked accent is a stigma, a mark of your status as immigrant or ignorant. During Caesar's reign, people went to classes to lose their accent, or more accurate to say, learn the right accent. At the same time, in the years before the World War II, ethnic comedians had their audiences rolling in the

---

[58] Franz Kafka, "Einleitungsvortrag über Jargon": <www.kafka.org/index.php?jargon>. Translation by Ernst Kaiser and Eithne Wilkins in *Dearest Father: Stories and Other Writings* (NY Schocken Books, 1954), pp. 382-383. However, in the citation I have translated "*Sprachgebilde* [literally speech-form] von Willkür und Gesetz" as "language's fabric of arbitration and law"; Kaiser and Wilkins's had "linguistic medley of whim and law."

aisles by performing their own and their audience's accents. This was the world of comedy Caesar came into. But it's one thing to make good fun with your own accent, another to mock the accents of others, which was also a staple of American ethnic comedy, which too often took an explicitly racist turn. Even if blackface performers identified with African-Americans, it did not undercut the racism of the appropriation. Mimicry always risks being heard as ridicule or mockery.

Doubletalk is usually considered something bad, deceitful, fraudulent. Saying one thing and meaning another, a means of disguising the true meaning of something. It is connected with viral Jewish stereotypes, all repeatedly invoked in Pound's 1941-1943 Radio Rome speeches[59]: the uprooted, usurpers of a language not rightly one's own, destroyers of the plain sense of the word and authenticity, untrustworthy, "diabolically clever."[60] Doubletalk is associated with gobbledygook, obfuscation, and gibberish— fake or counterfeit language, what George Orwell famously stigmatizes as doublespeak or bullshit, which gives "an appearance of solidity to pure wind."[61] It's the talk of carnival barkers, crooked politicians and kike lawyers, fascists and communists. It is nothing but bad faith.

---

[59] See my 1984 "Pounding Fascism (Appropriating Ideology, Mystification, Aestheticization, and Authority in Pound's Poetic Practice)," collected in *A Poetics* (Cambridge: Harvard University Press, 1992).

[60] Joseph Litvak, "Adorno Now," *Victorian Studies*, 44:1, 2001, p. 37. Litvak discusses the relation of Theodor Adorno's use of dialect to Jewish comedians, including Caesar, especially when they turn highfalutin language into gibberish, as, Litvak notes, Adorno does to Heideggerian lingo: "How many of these jokes, that is, show the reversal as, precisely, an effect of gesture, where gesture is the part of language that, like a provincial accent or an unassimilated parent, embarrasses language? That the embarrassment should strike at the very moment when language is most concerned to make a good impression accounts, of course, for the particular sting with which the jokes themselves strike. Just when language thinks it has everything, especially itself, under control, it starts gesturing, or even gesticulating, thereby hysterically displaying one of the classic signs of an always excessive Jewish identity."

[61] Orwell never uses the term "doublespeak" (or bullshit), though, in *1984*, he writes about "doublethink" and "new speak"; those two terms, combined, suggest *doublespeak*. In his 1946 essay against the decay and corruption of language, "Politics and the English Language," Orwell argues for clear language and against obfuscating writing styles, what he calls "swindles and perversions." In some circumstance, his views offer practical advice; in others, they become a method of policing language and enforcing normalization: <orwell.ru/library/essays/politics/english/e_polit/>.

Doubletalk begins in the deliberately unintelligible and fragmented. Modernist poetry has often been tarred with this brush. It's fast talking on theory and chock full of elisions and evasions, obscure references, logical lapses, emotional bankruptcy; in other words, *the kind of poetry I want*. Caesar saw the poetry in these language textures, even if he would have figured them as "material" not "poetry." In the immediate wake of the extermination of the European Jews, he practiced a kind of shtick alchemy, turning the Jewish stigmas of accent and shyster into song, in the process turning the tools of intolerance and nationalism on their heads. Doubletalk is applied nomadics (to use Pierre Joris's term for non-national language[62]): it pushes back against blood and soil nativism.

Two American Jews—Caesar and Milton Berle—were among the most popular TV entertainers in the U.S. in the years shortly following the Khurbn.[63] In the context of popular entertainment of the time, parodies of "foreign" languages and culture were common, ranging from racist ethnic parody and blackface to self-parodies that actively mocked stereotypes. It is a long way from Caesar to British Jewish comedian Sacha Baron Cohen's accent-heavy Ali G and Borat. Caesar was unlikely to offend his mass audience on grounds of cultural appropriation. Nonetheless, Jewish comedians walked a fine line between their antic hysteria and anti-Semitic stereotypes related to rootlessness, parasitism, vulgarity, and impurity.

In the realm of High Modernism, the cultural supremacism of Pound and Eliot turned their cultural appropriations into a virtue, something Zukofsky targeted, at least in respect to "The Waste Land," in his 1926 "Poem Beginning 'The.'" But virtue was not in the cards for the likes of Sid Caesar and his Jewish successors, from Jerry Lewis and Mel Brooks (born Melvin Kaminsky in 1926) to Don Rickles (1926), Jackie Mason (born Yacov Moshe Maza in 1931), Joan Rivers (born Joan Alexandra Molinsky in 1933), Larry David, and Sarah Silverman, nor his antic/anarchistic predecessors, the Marx Brothers and the Three Stooges. Much less for Rodney Dangerfield (born Jacob Cohen in 1921), who built his act around getting no respect.

---

[62] Pierre Joris, *A Nomad Poetics* (Wesleyan: Wesleyan University Press, 2003).

[63] *Khurbn* is a Yiddish word for destruction and is synonymous with *Shoah*, which is the Hebrew word for catastrophe.

If these outsider Jewish comedians risked mocking, albeit hilariously, conventional American sentimental norms, they often felt the need to show that in "real" life they were straight, well-adjusted Americans. The perfect realization of this is the split personality of Julius Kelp and Buddy Love in Jerry Lewis's 1963 film, *The Nutty Professor*. But it's there in the sycophantic sentimentality of Rickles when he stops his insult-shtick and gets personal with Johnny Carson (or, more accurately, launches into his ingratiation-shtick), just as it's there in Lewis's painfully sincere lounge singing and in his conspicuous philanthropy on his long-running, pity-inducing muscular dystrophy telethons. Significantly, Bruce had no "nice guy" alt. persona. In the age of reality TV, Rivers "personal" side spins into yet more crazy parody with *Joan & Melissa: Joan Knows Best?*, the title mocking the classic American situation comedy of enforced normalcy, *Father Knows Best*. David, in his most commercially successful enterprise, *Seinfeld*, had the super nice Jerry Seinfeld as his foil; he turned his masterpiece, *Curb Your Enthusiasm*, into a celebration of misanthropy.

Caesar walked the line and the toll on him was enormous. He sputtered out of control midway in his life, falling prey to the drugs and drink he used to keep himself going at maximum speed and precarious abandon.[64] Bruce's fall was more severe, dying of a heroin overdose at 40 in 1966, at the aesthetic height of his career. Bruce was just three years younger than Caesar. He was strictly downtown, nightclubs, intentionally offensive. In contrast, Caesar was mainstream, TV, intentionally inoffensive. Caesar's best work was over by 1958, when he was 36; after that, as he describes it, he was mostly on autopilot, with what he calls his "Dark Period" beginning in mid-60s. Like Caesar, Bruce started as Borscht Belt entertainer, but he went on to create polyvocal long-form talking essays (call them talks or talk poems), before becoming a martyr, persecuted by the state as morally repugnant. A master of doing "the

---

[64] Caesar suffered from violent manic outbursts, chronic anxiety, insecurity, and depression, with something like bulimia thrown in. It sounds bipolar. To curb his drinking, and for insomnia, his doctors prescribed pills, which he added to the booze. At various times, he was taking chloral hydrate, sodium amytal, amobarbital, Miltown, Placidyl, Equanil, and Seconal, all the while drinking heavily.— *Where Have I Been,* pp. 135, 148, 184. Caesar depicts the toll of drink in the beautiful Chaplin/Keaton silent film pastiche, "A Drunk There Was," *Caesar's Hour*, Jan. 16, 1956 <youtu.be/G76HrPTWj4I>.

police in different voices,"[65] Bruce's counter-culture genius has held up better than Caesar's commercial success.

In *Caesar's Hour*, as well as various late video interviews, Caesar repeats the same stories with the same spin, sometimes in a mechanical way, with only flashes of the spark that made him great. After starting his career on the wild and crazy side, in the last decades of his life he did all he could keep his story, and himself, straight.

Despite the essential sweetness of his on-screen performances, at the very height of his fame, Caesar felt a need to undercut the aesthetic and intellectual challenge of his work in order "humanize" himself, to show that the man behind the clown mask was not a vulgar, shrill, shtetl vaudevillian playing for easy laughs to the masses, not a queerly manic, doubletalking mongrel, not, that is *too Jewish*, but rather someone who had "class." He needed to show he was a "real man" interested in guns, a devoted husband and father, and also to "couth up" and show he was refined connoisseur of high art to boot— mixed messages that go with the striving for assimilation.

There is tremendous pathos in watching Edward R. Morrow's live TV interview with Caesar in his upscale Park Avenue apartment in a 1954 segment of *Person to Person*.[66] Sid kisses his daughter goodnight for the benefit of the national audience (she stayed up late so she could be on TV, he tells us). Caesar then takes Morrow into his gun room, which is decked out with rifles on a rack and a mounted deer's head. "I used to do a lot of hunting," says Sid, and goes on to tell the story of his snagging the deer, the only animal he has ever killed, so he says. The room looks like it was installed by the prop people on his show.[67] As he points to the deer head, it falls off from the wall and he holds it up for the rest of the segment,

---

[65] A draft title of Eliot's "The Waste Land" was "He Do the Police in Different Voices."

[66] "Sid Caesar on *Person to Person* with Edward R. Murrow," Oct 1, 1954: <writing.upenn.edu/ezurl/8>. Caesar's apartment at 940 Park Ave. (81st Street) was in one of the most exclusive neighborhoods in the U.S., in other words a WASP safe space. Such an apartment was the ultimate status symbol. My parents moved into a similarly decorated place around the same time, but on the less restricted Upper West Side.

[67] Caesar was physically imposing, gun-obsessed, and had a violent temper. He blew off steam shooting at tin cans with the rifles he collected and kept in the apartment.— *Where Have I Been*, p. 132, 196.

keeping a straight face. The entire show gives the sense of Caesar as a deer caught in the headlights. It would take almost fifty years for this public flagellation of the Jewish comedian to be exorcised by Rivers on *Joan & Melissa*. In the final segment of the *Person to Person* interview, Sid proudly shows Morrow a painting he owns by Maurice de Vlaminck, his "favorite" work in a collection that was inspired, he says, by reading *Lust for Life*, the Van Gogh biography by Irving Stone. Sid is something of an Impressionist himself, he tells Morrow, suppressing the punch line: *I do impressions.*

"I have an interest in art," Sid Caesar tells Edward R. Morrow and the millions watching at home.[68]

—*You bet your life you do.*

4. From the Basque

> Eragozpena aundiya dezu
> ta da aundienetakua.
> Auxe, bai, dala gaurko egunian
> estali gabe zulua

>> Ears are poppin' everybody's dancin'
>> to the Andalusiana.
>> Ax, bat, delirious bobbing especially
>> establishes gulled surfeit.

> Olaku leku biar biarrezkuan
> izenbat on ona egin leiken,
> antxen bilduta zuri ta beltzak!
> Ez da gauz erraza neurtzen.

>> O like a leaky bear's Bar Mitzvah
>> intent on owning, egging, lurking

---

[68] *Your Show of Shows* (1950-1954) and *Caesar's Hour* (1954-1957) introduced many of genres that were later picked up by *SCTV, Monty Python,* and *Saturday Night Live,* among many other shows. Caesar's parodies of other TV shows qualify as postmodernism under most definitions of the term. Indeed, Caesar was one of the first artists to create "born TV" work.

Anxious bickering surely taps ballistic!
As the gauze errata neutralizes.[69]

Other of my homophonic translations include "Click Rose for 21" from Dominique Fourcade's *Rose Declic* (1987); "Nuclear Blanks" after Esteban Pujals (1998); "Me Tranformo," after Régis Bonvicino (1999); "Laurel's Eyes" from Heine's "Die Lorelei" (1999), part of *Shadowtime*; "Death Fugue Echo" after Stefan Georg's "Maximin" (2006); Paul Celan's "Todtnauberg" (2009); and "Klang" after Peter Waterhouse (2016); but also two quasi-homophonic/homeomorphic translations, which retain much of the lexical sense of the source poems— *"The Maternal Drape" or the Restitution* from Claude Royet-Journoud's *'Le drap maternel' ou la restitution* (1984) and "Work Vertical and Blank" from Anne-Marie Albiach's "Travail Vertical et Blanc" (1989).[70]

5. a jew / among the Indians

In America, we exiled the native peoples as part of process of extermination, then endeavored to erase their languages from cultural memory. Early on Jerome Rothenberg, a Bronx native who came of age during the Khurbn, recognized himself as "a jew / among the Indians."[71] In 1968, he published *Technicians of the Sacred: A Range of Poetries from Africa, America, Asia, Europe, and Oceania*. Shortly after, with *The Horse Songs*, he introduced "total translation," which has close affinities with homophonic translation, carrying into the performance of the translation the "full" sound dynamic of the source text, including the vocables.[72]

---

[69] Jack Collom asked me to translate an unidentified poem from a newspaper. He collected several responses in *Olaku Leku Biar or A Leak on His Coffee-Colored Beret: Mistranslations from the Basque*, ed. Jack Collom: Privately printed by the editor in 1993, some copies reissued by Baksum Books (Boulder, CO, 2015). Basque, or Euskara, is the only language that carries over from pre-Roman southwest Europe.

[70] *"The Maternal Drape" or the Restitution* (Windsor, VT: Awede Press, 1984); "Click Rose for 21" in *The Sophist* (1987); "Laurel's Eyes" in *Shadowtime* (2005); "Death Fugue Echo" in *Girly Man* (2006); "Todtnauberg" in *Recalculating*.

[71] "Jerome Rothenberg: Double Preface," *Pitch of Poetry*, p. 162.

[72] Jerome Rothenberg, "Total Translation: An Experiment in the Translation of American Indian Poetry": <ubu.com/ethno/discourses/rothenberg_total.html>.

Rothenberg sought to bring the verbal art of analphabetic cultures into an active space of formally radical contemporary poetry. The question for him was not whether we have the right to translate the poetry of indigenous and non-alphabetic cultures but whether we have right not to. Up until that time, translations of this range of poetry focused more on plot than on sound, rhythm, and performance; this focus on content over form reflected the ideology of the translators and ethnologists and negated much of the culture they proposed to capture.[73] Rothenberg's commitment was to transcreation and transduction, sound writing and performance. He gathered midrashic translations for which process is commentary. The point was not to appropriate the source works but to enter into open-ended dialogs with them.

Ale modes fun iberzetsung, radikal nit mer vi kanvenshanal, fartrakhtn zikh di oryenteyshanz aun savs fun di transleyterz[74]: All modes of translation, radical no more than conventional, reflect the orientations and desires of the translators. And all translations are asymmetrical, both masking and revealing the discrepant cultural, economic, and political power of the translated and the translation. The ever-present danger is that the dominant party to the transaction is just toying with its object of affection and is aloof to, or incapable of, reciprocity. This is a pattern of supremacist exploitation that is repeated endless times. Yet, to refuse translation because too much is lost or distorted is to put purity above contamination and miscegenation. What or who gives the "right" to translate? If one translates works from within the Western canon, questions of appropriation do not arise. Except if you are viewed as a poacher or parasite, as Pound, Eliot, and legions of others, including Stalin, felt about rootless cosmopolitan Jews. As Eliot wrote, "Reasons of race and religion combine to make any large number of free-thinking Jews undesirable."[75]

---

[73] See Dennis Tedlock, "On the Translation of Style in Oral Narrative," *The Spoken Word and the Work of Interpretation* (Philadelphia: University of Pennsylvania Press, 1983).

[74] וזא זנאשייטנעירא יד רזי נטכאארטראפ, לאנאשנעוונאק יוו רעמ טינ לאקידאר, גנוצעזרעביא וזפ סעדאמ עלא זרעטיילסנארט יד וזפ סוואס.

[75] T. S. Eliot, *After Strange Gods: A Primer of Modern Heresy* (London: Faber and Faber, 1933, p. 20). Translator's note: In the Esperato, the Eliot quote was translated

For fundamentalist Jews, the people of the book means *just one book* (and the commentaries on this one book). "Free-thinking" Jews are the ones who have broken with nativist orthodoxy, moving beyond their immediate culture to imagine themselves as part of a larger world, as did Zukofsky and Mandelstam, Caesar and Rothenberg.[76] *Cosmopolitan* is a stigmatic code word for Jews as usurpers because it suggests global trafficking in cultural capital that doesn't belong to you, which only natives have the "right" to. Antinomian Jews are just one example of this phenomenon. African-American poet Melvin Tolson ran up against just such a wall when he strayed from what was considered his rightful cultural materials by adopting a "high-modern" style related to Eliot's *The Waste Land* rather than sticking to what were assumed to be his own indigenous cultural styles.[77]

There is nothing so beautiful nor more essential for communication, nothing so sacred, as the inauthentic becoming aware of itself.

6. on wind, should be written, on running water

If Sid Caesar was the most popular Jewish comedian of the 1950s, Louis Zukofsky (born in 1904) was among the most unpopular Jewish poets,

as "Kialoj de raso kaj religio kombinas fari ajnan grandan nombron de libera-pensado judoj nedezirindaj." On the other side of the political spectrum, the Soviet campaign against Jews as "rootless cosmopolitans" (безродный космополит, bezrodnyi kosmopolit) began immediately after World War II. A crackdown on Yiddish writers and poets followed, culminating in the state murder of leaders of the Jewish Anti-Fascist Committee on Aug. 12, 1952, commemorated as the "Night of Murdered Poets." "The trial of 1952 did more than wipe out some of the best Yiddish literary talents of the century; it completed the destruction of Yiddish in Europe."— Joseph Sherman, "Seven-fold betrayal: the murder of Soviet Yiddish," *Midstream* (2002): <www.thefreeli-brary.com/"Seven-fold betrayal": the murder of Soviet Yiddish.-a090332016>

[76] The break from the world of our parents is often traumatic. Zukofsky recounts his becoming other to his mother in "Poem Beginning 'The.'" In *Where Have I Been*, Caesar recalls his father's silence when he sees him, near death, in a specially arranged screening of *Tars and Spars*: "you say you make five hundred dollars a week?" (p. 73). I remember my father, in the hospital in his last days in 1977, listening to tape of a reading of mine, the only time he'd heard me, his disapproving silence melting, for a moment, into acknowledgement.

[77] See Michael Berubé, *Marginal Forces / Cultural Centers: Tolson, Pynchon, and the Politics of the Canon* (Ithaca: Cornell University Press, 1992).

overshadowed by official verse culture favorites Delmore Schwartz and Karl Shapiro (both born in 1913). Zukofsky's son Paul reports that his family first got a TV around 1951-1953 and that he remembers his mother recognizing a Yiddish word in one of Caesar's Japanese doubletalk routines, picking up on Caesar's boast.[78]

The most commonly cited origin for American homophonic translation is Louis and Celia Zukofsky's *Catullus*, written between 1958-1966 and published in 1969. Like the Hebrew homophonics in "*A*"-15, *Catullus* is not pure—glosses of the non-homophonic lexical meaning poke through at times, for example, where Zukofsky has *wind* for the Latin *vento* in *Catullus* 70.[79] The fact that English and Latin allow so many cognates, and because of many specific choices and tweaks by the Zukofskys, *Catullus* abounds with semantic echoes, puns, and commentaries on the source poems, while at the same time bringing the listener closer to the sound and syntax of the Latin. Homophonic translations from languages with less in common with English, such as Hebrew, Finnish, Chinese, Tamil, or Basque, pose different problems and open up other possibilities but up the uncanniness factor for apparent synchronicities.

Nulli se dicit mulier mea nubere malle
quam mihi, non si se Iuppiter ipse petat.
dicit: sed mulier cupido quod dicit amanti,
in vento et rapida scribere oportet aqua.

[CATULLUS 70]

Zukofskys:
Newly say dickered my love air my own would marry me all
whom but me, none see say Jupiter if she petted.

[78] Paul Zukofsky and Charles Bernstein, email exchange, Nov. 9, 2016. Mixing Yiddish into the Japanese doubletalk is a perfect example of Caesar's macaronics.

[79] For Latin versions of Catullus's poems see "The Poetry of Gaius Valerius Catullus": <en.wikibooks.org/wiki/The_Poetry_of_Gaius_Valerius_Catullus>. I included the Zukofskys' homophonic translation of 70 in the *Selected*, p. 158, along with my own translation of the poem, p. 172. The full set of the Zukofsky Catullus translations are collected in *Anew: Complete Shorter Poetry* (New York: New Directions, 2011). Lawrence Venuti wrote about this work in his indispensable *The Translator's Invisibility* (New York: Routledge, 1995).

Dickered: said my love air could be o could dickered a man too
in wind o wet rapid a scribble reported in water.

Here's my translation:
None, says my woman, would she want to marry more
than me, not if Jupiter himself insisted.
says: but what a woman says to a smitten lover,
on wind, should be written, on running water.[80]

In their homophonic translation of *Catullus* 85, the Zukofskys have
the non-homophonic anchor words *hate* and *love* in their translation.
Richard Tuttle and I moved through several versions of this poem, before selecting the last one (*Recalculating*, 136).

Odi et amo. quare id faciam, fortasse requiris.
nescio, sed fieri sentio et excrucior.

Zukofskys:
O th'hate I move love. Quarry it fact I am, for that's so re queries.
Nescience, say th' fierry scent I owe whets crookeder.

Bernstein/Tuttle:
Odious and amorous: Query: why'd I do that?
Don't know, just feelings & excruciating

•

Hating & loving. Hey: why's that?
Beats me, just my feelings & I'm crucified

•

Hate and love. Why's that?, you'd ask
Don't know, I feel it and it's torture.

"*A*"-15, was written in 1964. The second stanza begins with a homophonic translation from *The Book of Job*. Without critical exegesis, it
would be unlikely most readers would get the source as *The Book of Job*,

[80] Bernstein, *Near/Miss* (Chicago, University of Chicago Press, 2018).

just as most of Caesar's viewers would probably not have recognize *The Last Laugh* as the source of "The German General." Both Zukofsky and Caesar insisted that their work could stand on its own. And yet knowing the source adds an uncanny dimension and marks the works as echopoetics ("low o loam echo"). Like Caesar's doubletalk ("coeval yammer"), Zukofsky's homophonics is not pure but part of textual mixture. It's midrashic and antinomian, offering echoes of the sound of the Hebrew, but also a biting commentary on Job's "gall" in his whining neighing about the "cruel hire" that life has turned out to be. Jeff Twitchell-Waas tracked down the Hebrew source and transliteration (a.k.a homophonic rendering), to which I added the King James translation:

He neigh ha lie low h'who y'he gall mood

[Job 3:7] וֹב הֵנֵּה אוֹבַת-לֹא דוּמְלַג יְהִי אוּהַה הַלְיַלַה הֵנֵה

hine halaila hahu yehi galmud al-tavo renana vo

Lo, let that night be solitary, let no joyful voice come therein.

So roar cruel hire / Lo to achieve an eye leer rot off

[Job 7:7] בוֹט תוֹאָרְל יָנֵיע בוּשַׁת-אֹל יַיַח חוּר-יָכ רֹכֵז

zekhor ki-ruakh khayai lo-tashuv eini lirot tov:

O remember that my life is wind: mine eye shall no more see good.

Mass th'lo low o loam echo / How deal me many coeval yammer

[Job 7:16] יָמָי לֶבֶה-יָכ יָנֵּמְמ לַדָח הָיֵחָא סָלֹעְל-אֹל יַתְסאָמ

maasti lo-leolam ekhye khadal mimeni ki-hevel yamai

I loathe it; I would not live alway: let me alone; for my days are vanity.[81]

The third stanza of "A-15" begins with an echo of God's answer to Job from out of a whirlwind (Zukofsky hears "wind" and "His roar" in the Hebrew). God answers, "Who is this that darkeneth counsel by words without knowledge?" (KJV, 38:2). (Zukofsky hears "milling bleat doubt.") Perhaps homophonic translation, like typing without writing,

---

[81] Zukofsky, *Selected*, p. 114. Interlinear notation from Jeff Twitchell-Waas: <z-site.net/notes-to-a/a-15>. Twitchell-Waas dates the poem Oct. 3 to Dec. 1, 1964.

43

just scratches the surface: words without knowledge, blowin' in the wind, transient, a "cruel hire." Man up, says the big man to a despairing Job. But maybe Job knew what he was talking about. His words, even if they grind doubt, speak to diasporic peoples with more resonance than God's. Milling it into what? Poetry? Who is this, the Torah's God asks, who talks without accepting that the basis of knowledge must be grounded in God's nativism (in the "one" who "laid the foundations of the earth" [38:4])? Who is this who's got the "gall" to talk out of the top of the head and from all sides of the mouth.

—Let there be doubletalkers who "scribble" and "yammer" "in wind … reported in water"!

7. The Translation is Father to the Poem

The most striking work of American homophonic translation after the Zukofskys's *Catullus* comes from another Jewish poet, and a close reader of Zukofsky, David Melnick (born 1938). Melnick's 1975 *Pcoet* is a signal work of post-*zaum* sound writing. But it is Melnick's 1983 *Men in Aida* that is the breakthrough for homophonic translation. *Men in Aida* is a full-scale homophonic translation of the first two books of *The Illiad*, replete with echoes of contemporary San Francisco gay culture at the time of AIDS catastrophe. *Homo* comes home. Here's the opening passage, Homer's Greek first, then a transliteration, then Melnick (in bold), and finally the standard (heterophonic) translation. Melnick's is a strict, rather than loose, homophonic translation:

μῆνιν ἄειδε θεὰ Πηληϊάδεω Ἀχιλῆος
mênin aeide thea Pêlêïadeô Achilêos
Men in Aïda, they appeal, eh? A day, O Achilles!
SING, goddess, the anger of Peleus' son Achilleus

οὐλομένην, ἣ μυρί᾿ Ἀχαιοῖς ἄλγε᾿ ἔθηκε,
oulomenên, hê muri' Achaiois alge' ethêke,
Allow men in, emery Achaians. All gay ethic, eh?
and its devastation, which put pains thousandfold upon the
    Achaians,

44

πολλὰς δ᾽ ἰφθίμους ψυχὰς Ἄϊδι προῖαψεν
pollas d᾽ iphthimous psuchas Aïdi proïapsen
Paul asked if teach mousse suck, as Aïda, pro, yaps in.

hurled in their multitudes to the house of Hades strong souls

ἡρώων, αὐτοὺς δὲ ἑλώρια τεῦχε κύνεσσιν
hêrôôn, autous de helôria teuche kunessin
Here on a Tuesday. 'Hello,' Rhea to cake Eunice in.

of heroes, but gave their bodies to be the delicate feasting

οἰωνοῖσί τε πᾶσι, Διὸς δ᾽ ἐτελείετο7 βουλή,
oiônoisi te pasi, Dios d᾽ eteleieto boulê,
'Hojo' noisy tap as hideous debt to lay at a bully.

of dogs, of all birds, and the will of Zeus was accomplished

ἐξ οὗ δὴ τὰ πρῶτα διαστήτην ἐρίσαντε
ex hou dê ta prôta diastêtên erisante
Ex you, day. Tap write a 'D,' a stay. Tenor is Sunday.

since that time when first there stood in division of conflict

Ἀτρεΐδης τε ἄναξ ἀνδρῶν καὶ δῖος Ἀχιλλεύς.
Atreïdês te anax andrôn kai dios Achilleus.
Atriedes stain axe and Ron ideas 'll kill you.

Atreus' son the lord of men and brilliant Achilleus.[82]

Ron Silliman, a great proponent of Melnick, published his one and only homophonic translation in 1978, with Rilke's title "Duino Elegie" transformed into Silliman's "Do We Know Ella Cheese?," and the opening of the first elegy, "Wer, wenn ich schriee, hörte mich denn aus der

[82] David Melnick, *Men in Aida,* Book One (Berkeley: Tuumba Press, 1983) and Book Two (Editions Eclipse, 2002), online at <eclipsearchive.org> and, for the Greek text and standard translation, *The Chicago Homer* <homer.library.northwestern.edu>. Listen to the Greek recited by Stephen G. Daitz at <writing.upenn.edu/ezurl/9>, excerpted from The Society for the Oral Reading of Greek and Latin: <rhapsodes.fll.vt.edu/Greek.htm>. Transliterations from <tlg.uci.edu/help/TranslitTest.php >. "Ron" in the final cited line of Melnick's is presumably his friend Ron Silliman.

45

Engel /Ordnungen?" becoming "Where / when itch scree / hurt as much / Then how's their angle /or known gun?"[83]

Any overview of postwar North American radical translation practices also needs to give a place of honor to bpNichol's 1979 *Translating Translating Apollinaire*.[84] Nichol and a few friends, including Steve McCaffery and Dick Higgins, devised over 50 approaches to translating the first poem Nichol published, a 1964 impressionistic, sampled version of Apollinaire's iconic 1913 poem "Zone." There is one French phrase that runs throughout the versions, "soleil cou coupé" (sun throat cut; sun a cut neck; cutthroat sun; so lay, cool, coupé), the famous last line of "Zone," as well as two of the proper names from Apollinaire's poem—Simon and Icarus. The "sound translation" in Nichol's book (his phrase) is not of the Apollinaire poem but Nichol's early translation of that poem. This is the first instance I know of an English to English homophonic translation, though related forms of echopoetics are hardly new in the long history of poetry. That one French phrase becomes "soil hay coo coup hay" and Nichol's whole poem has a sound typical of homophonic translation.

First stanzas of Nichol's echoing of "Zone":

>   Icharrus   winging u p
>   Simon the Magician   from Judas   high in a tree,
>   everyone   reaching for the sun

---

[83] Ron Silliman, notes on homophonic translation from his blog, Aug. 30 and 31, 2003: <writing.upenn.edu/epc/authors/bernstein/syllabi/readings/silliman.html>.

[84] bpNichol, *Translating Translating Apollinaire: A Preliminary Report* (Milwaukee: Membrane Press, 1979), on-line at <bpnichol.ca/sites/default/files/archives/document/Translating%20Translating.pdf>. Also of note: *Six Fillious* by Nichol, Robert Filliou, McCaffery, George Brecht, Higgins, and Dieter Roth (Membrane Press, Milwaukee: 1978), in which a poem by Filliou is the seed for a chain of translations, none of which are homophonic; and *Rational Geomancy: The Kids of the Book-machine: the Collected Research Reports of the Toronto Research Group, 1973-82* by Nichol and McCaffery (Vancouver: Talon Books, 1992), which includes far-ranging discussions of radical approaches to translation.

                    great towers of stone
        built by the Aztec, tearing their hearts out
        to offer them, wet and beating

Nichol's "sound translation" of his "Zone" poem:

        hick or ass   was king cup
        Samantha   my chess yen   front   chew   deo   hyena tory,
        heavy Juan   Gris chin   guffaw earth son

                        Greta hours office tone
        bill to buy Thea's texts, terrier hard stout
        two hover then, whet tongue bee sting

In "Acoustic Room" (2000), Chris Tysh does a homophonic translation from the second of Lautréamont's *Les Chants de Maldoror*: "Allons,
Sultan, avec ta langue, débarrasse-moi de ce sang qui salit le parquet. Le
bandage est fini: mon front étanché a été lavé avec de l'eau salée, et j'ai
croisé des bandelettes à travers mon visage." becoming "All on, Sultan,
evoke two languages, debar us, my dizzy song key, sail / it o'er the parquet. The bandage is fine: man, front attention, hate / to lovey away; deal
o Sally, edgy crossy, this bandolier, a travesty / of my visage."[85]
    There is a comic dimension to these sound translations. Humor is a
fundamental structure of homophonic translation, even if done with a
straight face. In contrast, my homophonic translations of Georg, and
Celan, and my quasi-homophonic Royet-Journoud and Albiach, avert
comedy. From 2002 to 2007, Robert Kelly wrote a series of non-comic "homeophonic" (as he terms them) translations of Paul Celan called
"Earish."[86] In 2011, he published a homeophonic, and non-comic, translation of Friedrich Hölderlin called *Unquell the Dawn Now*.[87]
    Jean Donnelly's *Green Oil* is a homophonic, and non-comic, transla-
tion of Francis Ponge's *Pièces*. *Green Oil* is an elegant long poem made

[85] *Continuity Girl* (New York: United Artists, 2000). See Silliman's notes on homophonic translation. In later work, Tysh has done trancreations of Beckett and Genet.

[86] Robert Kelly, "Earish" <writing.upenn.edu/library/Kelly-Robert_Earish.html> and
<www.rk-ology.com/Earish_-_Paul_Celan.php>.

[87] Robert Kelly, *Unquell the Dawn Now* (New Paltz, NY: McPherson & Co, 2001).

up of short lines (eight sections of unrhymed couplets with no punctuation).[88] The work has the sharp torquing rhythm of Robert Creeley or George Oppen, but it is more semantically labyrinthine, bouncing off word associations and evocative enjambments. *Green Oil* would be unrecognizable as a homophonic translation since it has only slight traces of specifically French syntax or idiom. Donnelly provides few keys to specific sound associations between her poem and Ponge's:

> we lash a trop
> to meaning
>
> on it quells
> our touching
>
> docks of
> ravishing
>
> moments with
> magnificent
>
> characters
> like loons
>
> that enter
> water
>
> in sight of
> every word
>
> despite
> every word (47)

---

[88] Jean Donnelly, *Green Oil* (Colorado Springs: Further Other Book Works, 2014). The poems, she says, "began in the process of liberal homophonic readings and orthographical transcriptions" (p. 9).

As Maureen Thorsen points out in a review of the book, Donnelly's title "Green Oil" plays off Ponge's "La Grenouille" ("The Frog"):[89]

Lorsque la pluie en courtes aiguillettes
lords do squalls ply a court of aging
rebondit aux prés
that rebounds our praise

saturés, une naine amphibíe,
& saturates our *amphibian* impulse
une Ophélie
one Ophelia version

manchotte, grosse à peine comme le poing,
mangled gross & pained with being

… poète et se jette …
poets & suggestions[90]

Jonathan Stalling's 2011 work, *Yingelishi* 吟歌丽诗 (*Chanted Songs Beautiful Poetry): Sinophonic English Poetry and Poetics*, takes stock English phrases from a travel guide for Chinese speakers and provides homophonic Chinese versions. Stalling then uses the isophones for an opera libretto.[91] In the process, simple English phrases are transformed

---

[89] Maureen Thorson, "I Think We Are Alone Now," in *Open Letters Monthly*, Nov. 1, 2015: <openlettersmonthly.com/i-think-were-alone-now/>.

[90] "Green Oil," *Green Oil*, p. 49. I have braided the first lines of the poem with the source, Francis Ponge, "La Grenouille," in *Le Grand Recueil-Pièces* (Paris: Gallimard, 1961), p. 59.

[91] Jonathan Stalling, *Yingelishi* (Boulder: Counterpath Press, 2011) and the web site for the work: <jstalling.com/yingelishi.html>. See Jacob Edmund, "English and Yíngélìshī: Jonathan Stalling's Homophonic Translations" <jacket2.org/commentary/english-and-yingelishi> and <quarterlyconversation.com/yingelishi-and-grotto-heaven-by-jonathan-stalling>. Stalling talked about his work at the 5th Convention of the Chinese/American Association for Poetry and Poetics, at California State University, Los Angeles, Nov. 14, 2016. He has gone on to use the sinophonic written characters as a way to teach both English and Chinese.

into a narrative in Chinese: the quotidian English is transformed into lyrically fanciful Chinese. The stock phrase "Close your eyes" is homophonically rendered as Chinese; the Chinese isophone is, in turn, translated into English as "Jade dew appears as mourning memories." *English* becomes *Yingelishi*, which translates as "chanted beautiful poetry." The opera can be heard simultaneously as English or Chinese. For English speakers, the work creates a Chinese-sounding accent that is solemn and lyric, which for Stalling is meant to counter "yellow-face minstrelsy" (stereotyped Chinese accent in English, often used in racist ethnic comedy routines). If the English sinophonics are intentionally not comic, the Chinese homophonic translation is, since it produces, for Chinese listeners, a doubletalk mishmashed from "real" linguistic elements, perhaps a macaronic cousin to Caesar's doubletalk.

Cousins to the homophonic are the *homeographic* and *homeomorphic* (which might more broadly be called *parallelism*). "The 85 Project" by Robert Majzels, Claire Huot, Nathan Tremblay consists of transcreations of Chinese poems into 85 character English visual poems.[92] Majzels also has transcreations from the Hebrew of *The Song of Songs*. The "85" poems begin by translating each Chinese character into an English word, echoing Xu Bing's homeographic "Art for the People" (1999) and "Square Word" calligraphy, which designs English words as Chinese characters (block constellations of several letters). Yunte Huang's homeomorphic (word-for-word) *SHI: A Radical Reading of Chinese Poetry* provides literal, character-for-character, translation of classic Chinese poems.

Red, Green, and Black, my 1990 translation, with Olivier Cadiot, of a work of his, is an example of what I mean by homeomorphic.

Dirk Weissmann, the co-organizer of the "Sound / Writing" conference, points to Ernst Jandl's early 1960s "oberflächenübersetzung" ("surface translation") as another early example of homophonic translation, in this case from English to German.[93] Jandl turns Wordsworth's "My heart leaps up when I behold / A rainbow in the sky" into "mai hart lieb zapfen eibe hold / er renn bohr in sees kai" and "The Child is father

---

[92] "The 85 Project": <85bawu.com>.

[93] Dirk Weissmann, "Übersetzung als kritisches Spiel: Zu Ernst Jandl's *oberflächenübersetzung*," *Das Spiel in der Literatur*, ed. Philipp Wellnitz (Berlin: Frank und Timme, 2013).

of the Man" into "seht steil dies fader rosse mähen." Perhaps we could translate this famous line back into the American as "see this upright, faded horse mowing," which is uncannily close to Wordsworth's meaning. The translation is father to the poem.

For *Shadowtime*, I made a homophonic translation of Jandl's "der und die" (1964).[94] Here are the first two lines, braided (the work is both homophonic and homeographic):

```
can dew and die can and die can tie his sin tap and
kam der und die kam und die kam vor ihm ins tal und
the war dew hoe and die has him and her and tar the
das war der ort und die sah hin und her und tat das
```

Voice recognition software brings another dimension to the homophonic. In *Hearing Things*, British deaf poet Aaron Williamson used voice recognition software to dictate/transcreate poems. Williamson speaks but can't hear his own voice. He describes the results as "deaf gain" in contrast to "hearing loss": "Why had all the doctors told me that I was losing my hearing, and not a single one told me that I was gaining my deafness?"[95] Within the larger context of the poetics of disability, I call this *deficit gain*, which might be a useful frame for the poetics of homophony and sound-alikeness. The title of one of Williamson's poems is "Geomancy," suggesting reading meaning into verbal scatter. Geomancy and deficit gain both resonate with homophonics, though it's essential to remain chary about eliding the circumstances of disabled people with terms for poetics.

> … You need to bend to listen, further to hear. … Feeble
> configurations skid out of forced swoons and dives, frail

---

[94] First published, with Jandl's original, in *Reft and Light: Poems by Ernst Jandl with Multiple Versions by American Poets* (Providence: Burning Deck, 2000). Juliette Valery did a French translation that begins— "pût eau tel tué pût tel tué pût lie son mal bat tel."

[95] Introduction" in H-Dirksen L. Bauman and Joseph J. Murray, eds., "*Deaf Gain: Raising the Stakes for Human Diversity* (Minneapolis: University of Minnesota Press, 2014), p. xv.

transport for the ear to zoom in and make something at
will. Marks to the paper arc your prostrate conclusions
yet your veiled head dullens design against any end at all.
...[96]

Pierre Joris tested the possibilities of voice recognition software in a
different way. He emailed me about it while I was in Paris for the "Sound
/ Writing" conference and staying at Hotel Des Grandes Hommes, where
André Breton and Philippe Soupault employed "automatic writing" to
compose *Magnetic Fields* in 1919. Joris read the French poem aloud into
his computer's "MacSpeech Dictate" application, which was set to tran-
scribe from English. Here is a bit of what he got (what was dictated followed by the computer transcription), with its wry evocation of the bad
student of French (such as I was) taking dictation during class:

LA GLACE SANS TAIN

Prisonniers des gouttes d'eau, nous ne sommes que des
animaux perpétuels. Nous courons dans les villes sans
bruits et les affiches enchantées ne nous touchent plus.
À quoi bon ces grands enthousiasmes fragiles, ces sauts
de joie desséchés? Nous ne savons plus rien que les astres
morts; nous regardons les visages; et nous soupirons de
plaisirs. Notre bouche est plus sèche que les pages per-
dues; nos yeux tournent sans but, sans espoir. Il n'y a plus
que ces cafés où nous nous réunissons pour boire ces
boissons fraîches, ces alcools délayés et les tables sont plus
poisseuses que ces trottoirs où sont tombées nos ombres
mortes de la veille.[97]

[96] From Aaron Williamson, "Geomancy" in *Hearing Things* (London: Bookworks,
2001), p. 22. Michael Davidson discusses Williamson's work in *Concerto for Left
Hand: Disability and the Defamiliar Body* (Ann Arbor: University of Michigan Press,
2008), pp. 87-93.

[97] André Breton, *Oeuvres Complèt* I (Paris: Gallimard, 1966), p. 106.

Please are the big good door, no one is so did it anymore
will be to period. No: only if he'd sown wheat in a set fiche
are shown being and pushed crude. Aqua balls into all on
Tuesday I submit IG unit, six cylinders what do I think?
Knew several people he and Kerry Seth Amo; no load up
on a recession; in whose appeal to pity he. Not put Bush at
2/good/bad dude; knows you ~ Psalm bitch, saws as well.
The reactor due to think deftly when will they be so bold
whilst they were so fresh, since I go in the 8880 tablets and
replaced it is ethical to our slumped on being a zone while
not that EA period.

In 1999, Richard Caddel did a "loose phonic version" of the early me-
dieval Welsh poem "Y Gododdin" by Neirin (or Aneurin). Here is #75,
braided with the Welsh poem of that same number, which, however, is
not necessarily the source:

earthly songs with common refrains
Ardyledawc canu kenian kywreint
loud lodger-bird by dizzy want
Llawen llogell byt bu didichwant
how many in hill bird idle amount
Hu mynnei engkylch byt eidol anant
every great march a mead feathering
Yr eur a meirch mawr a med medweint
forgetting the airing when fainting
Namen ene delei o vyt hoffeint / Kyndilic aeron wyr enouant[98]

---

[98] Richard Caddel, "For the Fallen," *Angel August* 16 (Jan. 1999):
< poetrymagazines.org.uk/magazine/record9ed3.html?id=13867>; *Y Gododin: A Poem
on the Battle of Cattraeth* (1852 edn): <gutenberg.org/files/9842/9842-h/9842-h.htm>.
Andrew Duncan, in his "Note" on Caddel's "phonic version," suggests that the text of
Y Gododin comes to us as sound echoes of a possible original rather than as a lexically
accurate version— "Ifor Williams' introduction to his edition points out the nature of
the text as we have it, where phonetic drift and association have taken over parts of the
original text": <poetrymagazines.org.uk/magazine/record82c5.html?id=13917>. In
Wild Honey Press's chapbook of the complete series (Dublin, 2000), which is presented
as an elegy for his son, Caddel offers various approaches to *Y Gododin*.

In more recent years, there has been a proliferation of novel translation practices, multilectical poetry, and poetry written by second-language speakers of English who live in non-English speaking places. Caroline Bergvall—a British/French/Norwegian poet—has been creating a mixed language or loose or macaronic homophonic poetry: doubletalking in Middle and Old English. *Meddle English* is Bergvall's remarkable Chaucerian vocal insinuations and extensions. In these layered excavations of Middle English, the old literally melts into the new, dwelling in the space between languages, which for her is not an abstraction but an embodying/enveloping ground. Moving from but burrowing into ESL/PSL (English/poetry as a second language), Bergvall's bravura performances move toward a fluid third term, not bilingual but n-lingual, as in the final section of "Crop," woven with permutations of an English phrase in Norwegian and French.

Some never had a body to call their own before it was taken
   away
som aldri hadde en kropp de kunne kalle sin egen før den ble
   revet bort
ceux dont le corps d'emblée leur est arraché

Some never had a chance to feel a body as their own before it
   was taken away
som aldri fikk oppleve en kropp som sin egen før den ble revet
   bort
ceux dont le corps d'emblée leur est arraché

Some never had a chance to know their body before it was taken
   away
som aldri fikk kjenne sin kropp før den ble revet bort
ceux dont le corps méconnu d'être arraché

Some were never free to speak their body before it was taken up
   and taken away
som var aldri frie til å si sin kropp før den ble løftet opp og revet
   bort
ceux dont le corps est arraché

Some tried their body on to pleasure in it before it was taken up
    beaten violated taken away
som tok sin kropp på for å nyte den før den ble løftet opp slått
    krenket revet bort
sont ceux au corps choppé violé arraché[99]

Bergvall's is an echopoetics of the "nomadic" and "disfluency," where blockages, stuttering, error, code switching, and skips are not fragments of a lost whole but stitches that make up a fabric. In *Meddle English* the frogs in our throats become catnip. This work continues with *Drift* (Nightboat, 2014) with its extensions, samplings, warpings, and deformations of the Old English of "The Seafarer," connecting the work of sound writing to migrancy and to the fate of refugees.

8. Wee Da Sign

Benny Lava is a YouTube video from 2007 that has clocked 7 million views.[100] Like Caesar's doubletalk, it is an example of a wildly popular work, not identified with poetry, that nonetheless has striking similarities to the mostly unpopular, if not to say deeply obscure, homophonic transcreations of the Zukofskys, Melnick, Bergvall, and others.

Benny Lava is based on a music video for the Tamil song "Kalluri Vaanil" from the 2000 Indian Tamil movie *Pennin Manathai Thottu*, with homophonic subtitles added by Mike Sutton (Buffalax). "The name Benny Lava comes from Sutton's homophonic translation of the Tamil lead line 'Kalluri vaanil kaayndha nilaavo?' as 'My loony bun is fine, Benny Lava!'"[101]

This is the beginning of the full text of homophonic subtitles, which is provided, in full, on the YouTube page:

    My loony bun is fine Benny Lava!

[99] "Caroline Bergvall, "Crop" in "Cropper," *Meddle English* (New York: Nightboat, 2011), pp. 147-148. There is a recording of Bergvall reading this passage on her PennSound page.

[100] "Benny Lava": <youtu.be/sdyC1BrQd6g>.

[101] "Pennin Manathai Thottu," *Wikipedia* <en.wikipedia.org/wiki/Pennin_Manathai_Thottu>.

Minor bun engine made Benny Lava!
Anybody need this sign? Benny Lava!
You need a bun to bite Benny Lava!
Have you been high today?
I see the nuns are gay!

This comic video is considered an example of a genre called Soramimi (from the Japanese 空耳, mishearing, literally "air ear") or *soramimi kashi* (空耳歌詞, mishearing lyrics). The homophonic process foments a proliferation of puns, double entendres, and off references and brings to mind Sid Caesar's comment that one of the sources of his verbal acrobatics, from when he worked in the Borscht Belt, was the jokes he and his friends made with misunderstandings between Yiddish and English. Kenneth Goldsmith's 2002 "Head Citations"—his comic compilation of misheard song lyrics—come to mind as another work based on mishearing, or let's just say where mishearing becomes rehearings becomes new hearings.[102]

There are other examples of popular homophonic videos.

Skwerl ("How English sounds to non-English speakers") is a 2011 short video by Karl Eccleston and Brian Fairbair in which the dialogue is done in English doublespeak.[103]

There is a related genre, where singers make up lyrics to pop songs without knowing the actual words or language.[104] In French, this is called *chanter en yaourt* and *yaourter*. The best-known example of this is Italian superstar Adriano Celentano's 1972 comic and delightfully pulsing song (and later TV clip), "Prisencolinensinainciusol," which is in English doublespeak. When you first hear it, it sounds like an American post-Elvis, pop song, punctuated by "all right!" The rollicking video

[102] Kenneth Goldsmith, "Head Citations": <writing.upenn.edu/epc/authors/goldsmith/works/head_citations.html>.

[103] Brian and Karl, *Skwerl*: <brianandkarl.com/SKWERL>. The shooting script is at <brianandkarl.tumblr.com/post/110560981278/we-get-a-lot-of-emails-asking-for-the-skwerl>.

[104] Caesar, Reiner, and Morris do something like this in 1956 and 1957 with their recurring rock band parody group "The Haircuts," making up "nonsense" lyrics, as Caesar calls them in *Where Have I Been,* p. 160.

has Celentano (born in 1938) as swinging, hip professor, giving a lesson, perhaps on global asymmetries to a class of schoolgirls seated as desks (the one prop is a globe).[105] Gramsci's "Some Aspects of the Southern Question" this is not. But it does express the global desire to be an American pop icon and Celentano plays the role, and has the sound down, better than most American pop stars.

YouTube user "orangebroomhead" has done a transcription of the song as if it was in English:

> You're the call may the say one
> Prisencolinensinainciusol ol all right
>
> Wee da sign nah shoes now da whole baby scene
> then a whole rate maybe give de collar bus die
> Brrrr, chance in my head begin the coal-hold
> Baby just teh-yeh bush joe hoe ... [106]

LyricWiki offers a quite different transcription, which makes no attempt to hear it as English. Indeed, it reads something like sound poetry or *zaum*:

> In de col men seivuan
> prisencolinensinainciusol all right
>
> Uis de seim cius nau op de seim
> Ol uait men in de colobos dai
> Trrr - ciak is e maind beghin de col
> Bebi stei ye push yo oh ...[107]

[105] Adriano Celentano, "Prisencolinensinainciuso": <youtu.be/-VsmF9m_Nt8>.

[106] "Prisencolinensinainciusol (Lyrics) (English translation)": <youtu.be/6bc7Bu-Li1kw≥>. Line breaks follow the LyricWiki transcription.

[107] "Adriano Celentano: Prisencolinensinainciusol Lyrics," LyricWiki: <lyrics.wikia.com/wiki/Adriano_Celentano:Prisencolinensinainciusol>. Mark Liberman's Language Log alerted me to this song: <languagelog.ldc.upenn.edu/nll/?p=1838>.

Benny Lava is either funny or offensive, maybe both. Does it appropriate and caricature, mocking the original language in a proud display of ignorance and condescension, is it a new kind of ethnically demeaning humor? Or is does it use a homophonic procedure to create a virtual space of lingua franca, a non-national overlay of languages? In other words, who is the joke on? Stalling's sinophonic translations are meant, he says, to counter the stereotyping of Chinese accents in English, though for Chinese speakers he has created a kind of whiteface. Caesar's good humor manages to make his doubletalking *laughing with* not *at*, except, and this exception is the rule, with Nazi doubletalk, where there is, still, plenty of good humor, an (un)leavening humor. But as a Jewish commercial entertainer, Caesar's approach has to lead to ingratiation, bathos, and charm: the clown telling jokes. And that's a lead hard to turn into gold.

Zukofsky remains rebarbative, inaccessible, and decidedly not ingratiating: difficulty that stays difficult. In this light, Zukofsky's poetry is a kind of doubletalk—an act on, as well in, English, kissing cousin to Zukofsky's older European contemporary, Paul Celan.

For Caesar, homophonic translation begins in bad faith and ends in the communal song of laughter. For Zukofsky, the sincerity and objectification of homophonic translation offers a way to reveal the truth in the materials of language, to make a deeper connection or fraternity between translated and translation. That is, not to begin with an original and then make a faithful copy, which is always a betrayal; but rather, to begin with an original and then make a cousin or clone or, indeed, *an* 'other' original. Homophonic translation becomes a way to counter the bad faith inherent in conventional (*heterophonic*/hegemonic), translation; that is to say, the replacement of one meaning complex with another, a replacement that often entails erasing the mark or stigmata of translation in an attempt to make the translation feel seamless or fluent.

In *Meddle English,* Bergvall puts it this way:

> I repeat what many have said, that poetic or art language
> must not implicitly be held to account of identities and
> national language, the seductions of literary history, or the
> frequently fetishistic methodologies of art movements, but
> rather seek, far and close, the indicators and practices of
> language in flux, of thought in making: pleasured language,

pressured language, language in heated use, harangued language, forms of language revolutionized by action, polemical language structures that propose an intense deliberate reappraisal of the given world and its given forms.[108]

Zukofsky and Melnick are not likely to offend classical Greeks or Latins or Rome-anians (as Caesar puns in a 1964 sketch). But this is perhaps what separates unpopular poetry with mass-market comedy and commercial entertainment.

The dialectal power relation in translation, who's on top or what's dominant, source or target, cannot be abolished by poetic fiat. The promise of the homophonic sublime is always imaginary, or, perhaps to say, a fantasy of the imaginary.

---

[108] Caroline Bergvall, "the meddle," from *Meddle English*, p. 17. Excerpt in *Sybil* (May 30, 2011) <sibila.com.br/english/caroline-bergvall/4785>

CHARLES BERNSTEIN is the winner of the 2019 Bollingen Prize for *Near/Miss* (University of Chicago Press, 2018) and for lifetime achievement in American Poetry. He is the author of over twenty-five books of poetry and essays, including *Topsy--Turvy* (2021), *Pitch of Poetry* (2016), and, in 2020, a collaboration with Ted Greenwald, *The Course*. The Donald T. Regan Professor, Emeritus, Department of English at the University of Pennsylvania, he lives in Brooklyn.